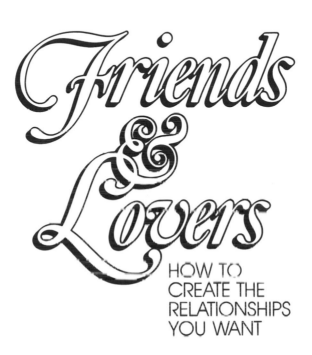

Friends & Lovers

HOW TO CREATE THE RELATIONSHIPS YOU WANT

MARC ALLEN

Whatever Publishing, Inc.
San Rafael, California

Published by Whatever Publishing, Inc.
58 Paul Drive, San Rafael, CA 94903

86 87 88 89   6 5 4 3 2

Cover design by Kathleen Vande Kieft

Photo by Edwin W. Smith

This book is dedicated to all my friends and lovers, past and present, for you have all been my best teachers, and I couldn't have written this without you....

To love is good; to love is difficult. For one human being to love another is perhaps the most difficult of all our tasks, the ultimate, the work for which all other work is but preparation.

For this reason young people, who are beginners in everything, cannot yet know love: they must learn it. With their whole being, with all their forces, they must learn to love. But learning-time is always a long, secluded time, and so loving, for a long while ahead and far on into life, is solitude....Love is at first not anything that means merging, giving over, and uniting with another; it is a high inducement to the individual to ripen, to become something in himself or herself.

Only in this sense, as the task of working on themselves, might young people use the love that is given them.

—Rainer Maria Rilke
Letters to a Young Poet

CONTENTS

INTRODUCTION

Today, well over 50 million people in America live alone, and do not enjoy the benefits of an intimate personal relationship.[1] For a very few special people this is an ideal way to live, but for far too many others, it is not. Of the vast numbers of people *involved* in intimate personal relationships, many are still not satisfied, not getting what they need. Significant relationships with others — family, friends, co-workers, neighbors — are strained, tensions remain unexpressed and unreleased for years, even a lifetime, and the resolution of these problems appears to be difficult, if not impossible, to achieve.

This book is for all those who want to create better, more meaningful relationships with the people in their lives. It presents proven principles and techniques that can help you create satisfying relationships with lovers and friends. These principles apply to all kinds of relationships, including family, work, social, and even political relationships. The techniques presented in this book have been tested in the laboratory of my own personal experience, and have consistently led to more open communication and more satisfying interactions with the people in my life.

The effects of these techniques can be just as rewarding for businesses, and even nations. In particular, the techniques presented in Chapter Four, "The Fine Art of Communication," if implemented by businesses or governments, could lead to far more productive businesses and even a world in which there is no need to go to war. But perhaps that is the subject of another book.

It is best to begin at the level of personal relationships — our friends and lovers. Once these relationships are working harmoniously for everyone involved, we can then move on to improving broader social relationships. Seldom do parents or schools teach effective methods for meeting lovers and companions, creating satisfying friendships, and sustaining personal relationships. I've never heard of a class, for instance, on effective communication for lovers. Yet these things are certainly of great importance in almost everyone's life.

This book presents solid, practical information that can help you develop your skill in a great art: the art of creating successful relationships. In the long run, time spent reading this book and experimenting with some of its techniques can not only make your personal life much more rewarding, but can actually make your world a better place to be. The only way to prove the truth of this claim is to try it, and see for yourself.

Friends and Lovers is not intended to be an exhaustive, detailed book that covers every contingency in life. You won't find specific advice on what to do when your baby (whether a child or a so-called grownup) is screaming in the middle of the night. You won't find specific advice on dealing with heartbreak, loneliness, or the other slings and arrows of our own individual fortune or fate or creation.

What you *will* find are basic, simple techniques that will help you deal with all these different problems *at their source*. The most important information in this book is contained in two processes which are presented at length: one helps you focus on yourself, the "core belief process," and the other helps you communicate more effectively with everyone else in your life. At the most basic level, all of our problems — *all* — can be dealt with effectively by (1) examining, and if necessary *changing*, our core beliefs about the problem, and (2) communicating with others in a skillful way.

Some of you may not agree with this. What about the *big* problems in the world? What about war? What about the nuclear threat? These are good questions — and I'm convinced that these big problems are identical to our own "little" problems, except they are magnified about four billion times.

Consider this possibility: The threat of nuclear war is here because (1) almost everybody believes that it has to be this way, that we *must* have the protection of a nuclear deterrant, meaning nuclear weapons, and (2) countries are not communicating effectively with each other. If they were, there would be no need for nuclear arms or war in the first place. The first reason involves core beliefs; the second involves communication. (For those of you who think all of this is nonsense, or want to explore this further, I recommend reading *How to Stop Believing in War* by Will Whittle.[2])

As I stress, repeatedly: You do not have to *believe* anything you read in this book. All you need to do is try a few of the exercises, especially the core belief process and the communication game, and judge for yourself.

A Note about Grammar

In order to have nonsexist grammar, avoiding constant use of "he" and "him" (or "she" and "her") to represent "he or she" and "him or her," some of the current rules of grammar must be relaxed. Otherwise, we have to endure bulky sentence construction (such as: "If your lover doesn't feel like doing what *he or she* promised to do, try to accept it and give *him or her* permission to do what *he or she* wants to do instead"), or resort to using the plural "they," a practice that is not only awkward, but is currently considered incorrect (i.e., "If your lover doesn't feel like doing what *they* promised to do, try to accept it and give *them* permission to do what *they* want to do instead").

When I could not avoid using one or the other of these forms, I generally chose the third-person plural because it is a bit smoother than the other, and it is now gaining increased acceptance. I hope readers who are sensitive to proper grammar will understand. At the rate grammar is changing, the time may soon arrive when this convention will be considered an acceptable way to avoid sexism in writing.

1

CREATING THE RELATIONSHIPS YOU WANT

The saying, "As we think in our hearts, so are we," not only embraces the whole of our being, but is so comprehensive as to reach out to every condition and circumstance of life. We are literally what we think, our character being the complete sum of all our thoughts. As the plant springs from the seed, so every act of ours springs from the hidden seeds of thought. A man or a woman is a growth by law, not a creation by artifice, and such cause-and-effect is as absolute and undeviating in the hidden realm of thought as in the world of visible and material things....[1]

—James Allen

A Changing World

IF YOU ARE READING this book, chances are good that you're either having difficulty meeting that "right" person, or you're feeling that some of the more important relationships in your life leave something to be desired. There may be many reasons for this, of course, reasons

13

involving yourself, others, and the world in general. Every day, your beliefs are reinforced by what you see around you. Without being consciously aware of it, perhaps, your beliefs have become set, firm, and relatively unchanging over the years.

Yet we live in a changing world, and we ourselves are changing, constantly. Biologists have demonstrated that even our basic cellular structure is in a constant state of flux. In fact, every seven years we have an entirely different body, for during this period of time all our old cells have been replaced by new ones. And, on an even deeper level, physicists have shown that our minds and bodies, composed of molecules, atoms, and subatomic particles, are in a constant state of movement and change. Change is the reality of our being; change is the nature of existence.

If our bodies and our world are changing all the time, which is certainly the case, then it must also be possible to change our *beliefs* about ourselves and our world, *and thus change ourselves and our world as a result.* By working on our personal belief structure, we can consciously direct the course of this change, and create a more desirable life experience for ourselves. This, in a nutshell, is the most important theme of this book.

It is not necessary to *believe* any of these ideas or theories. You only have to dare to try something new, experiment a bit. Try some of the exercises which follow, with as open a mind as possible, and see what happens for you. Don't simply accept what I say (or what anyone else may say, for that matter) as truth, until you have tested it in the laboratory of your personal experience. Then form your own conclusions. These ideas and techniques have evolved from both my experiences and those of my friends and lovers over the last decade or more.

The basis of this book came from the constant trial and error of daily life, and it was written because these ideas and techniques are *working effectively* for me, and for my lover, friends, and business associates. Just as these ideas and techniques have been developed and tested through my personal experience, so they can only be grasped, and used effectively, through your personal experience.

All that is needed is an open mind. Just as every scientist must do, you have to open yourself up to the possibility that you and your world really might be quite different from your current conceptions. So go ahead — open up to the idea of entertaining different possibilities; open up to the idea of change. It can be scary at times, because most of us feel threatened by change, even change for the better, yet it is time for a change, individually and globally. Look at it as an adventure, a great experiment — an experiment that can improve your life and your relationships, and even your world. Who knows what you will discover? Maybe you'll find yourself stepping into a phone booth, tearing off your old clothes, and emerging as a superhero! Anything is possible. Maybe you'll even find yourself creating a wonderful, even an *ideal*, relationship, and living in a peaceful world, finding complete satisfaction in everything you do.

It can be done, but first, some inner work is necessary, something you do yourself, alone. You must prepare yourself psychologically, by clearing away some of the major psychological "blocks" you have created for yourself. It is entirely personal work and this inner work must be done before you will see any outward changes. This first step of psychological preparation is absolutely necessary in order to achieve the quality of life promised by this book: a life filled with the kind of relationships you want to have, and a lifestyle in which you are surrounded by people that have one thing in common: supportive, successful relationships with each other.

I encourage you to take the time to work, and *play*, with the following material. Take your time, read slowly and thoughtfully, feel free to browse around in it, and try some of the exercises. Take the time to question and challenge this material, and question and challenge yourself. It will be time well spent.

Clearing Psychological Blocks

Everyone of us has a number of "psychological blocks," or neuroses, that affect some aspect of our attitudes or behavior. Each one of these blocks is based on various fears that we have developed during our lives. We experience these neuroses each time we hold ourselves back, failing to grow and develop as far as we can or to enjoy our lives as fully as we can. These blocks are obstacles to realizing our greatest potential in life, because they prevent us from taking risks, trying new things, and making positive changes in our lives.

Everyone is neurotic to some degree — those who claim they have no neuroses whatsoever are deceiving themselves. It is important, however, to distinguish between neurosis and *psychosis:* psychosis is extreme behavior that impairs a person's ability to function as a capable, responsible human being. Not too many people, fortunately, have gone to the extreme trouble of creating a state of psychosis for themselves. Neurosis, on the other hand, is found in all the little doubts, worries, hesitations, and fears that inhibit us, in all the places where we show a lack of self-esteem or are overly critical of ourselves or others, and so on. In fact, much of what we call "normal" behavior is really neurotic behavior: worrying parents, frustrated kids, highly stressful work environments are all situations we accept as "normal," even inevitable. Yet these situations can be changed. There is no universal law that says parents have to worry, kids have to be frustrated and rebellious, or work environments have to be stressful.

These neuroses, these "blocks," can be changed; the challenge is to first take an honest look at them, and then let them go and move beyond them. The process is not difficult, but it does require a willingness to change, to let go of old, familiar habit patterns, and it takes a certain degree of persistence to establish new, healthier habit patterns.

If you aren't creating satisfying relationships in your life, you can be sure you've got some psychological blocks to overcome. You've got some neuroses you need to look at and let go of. It can be done.

The First Step: Acceptance

The first step in this process is often overlooked, but so necessary: the first step is *acceptance of yourself*. If you can accept yourself as you are now, you'll find it a lot easier to change for the better. *It is all right to be neurotic,* and you have a lot of company — nearly the entire human race, in fact. Actually, neuroses serve a useful function: they keep us discontent, and so we are forced to examine ourselves, which is necessary in order to improve our situation, to grow and develop, and, eventually, to become stronger, clearer, able to fulfill our greatest potential in life.

Accept yourself, as you are now, at this moment. Ask yourself if there are things about yourself that you are not accepting, things you feel guilty or angry or fearful about. Honestly look at each one of these things, one at a time, and mentally embrace each one as being, for the present, an acceptable part of you. All these things have been necessary for your development so far, and they are okay. Accept them, and you'll find it much easier to eventually let them go.

Accept your friends and lovers, as they are, too. Accept your parents and family, your boss and your co-workers. Accept everyone you come in contact with. Everyone of us is doing the best we can. Acceptance does not mean that you have to put up with anything you don't feel good about, or that you can't express your honest feelings to others. Quite the contrary: once you thoroughly accept yourself and others, you'll find it much easier to give honest feedback, and this feedback is effective, for it is readily heard. (We'll discuss this in detail in the next chapter.)

Though it is difficult for a great many of us, it is far better for our mental health and our effectiveness in the world to learn to accept our world as it is, too. Sometimes it's hard for me to accept, I'll admit. When I read in the newspapers about the constant violence in the world, all the forms of brutality we human beings practice on each other, the atomic weapons we continue to build, or the chemical wastes and pollution we've created, I sometimes find myself reacting angrily, or with a deep sadness. It *is* difficult to accept what is happening in the world today. Yet a quieter, wiser part of me knows that I have to accept the world as it is, at least for now. Of course this is not to say that I can't and won't try to change it for the better. I'll continue to support the groups I support and write the letters and books I write, and I'll continue to explore new ways to have a positive effect in the world. But I have to accept it, here and now, for what it is. It may seem paradoxical, but this acceptance puts me in a much stronger position to change things for the better. And it's better for my physical and mental health, too. This is true whether I'm dealing with myself, my relationships, or my world. So the first step toward making effective change is to accept things as they are.

Core Beliefs

If you're still reading, if the fact that we have to accept the unacceptable hasn't put you off, then you're ready for the next step toward creating healthy, satisfying relationships. So far, we have considered the fact that we are all somewhat neurotic, and we have seen how we create psychological blocks that prevent us from attaining what we truly want for ourselves and our world. Next, it is essential to determine the *cause* of our neuroses. What is at the root of our psychological blocks? Once we find the cause, we have taken a giant step toward the cure. A great many teachers, religious leaders, those in the helping professions, scientists, philosophers, intellectuals, writers, and other frustrated individuals have tried to answer this question. A great many theories have been enumerated: the cause of our problems is basically due to environment, or heredity; problems are also blamed on parents, genetic coding, sexual energy, cultural heritage, physical defects, mental defects, emotional instability, sins we have committed, a basic lack of understanding, or a myriad of other reasons that a great many creative (and sometimes desperate) imaginations have devised.

But these theories blame factors beyond our control — and it is very difficult to change things that are beyond our control. It is difficult to change our environment (especially our *early* environment, which is now a thing of the past), or our defects, and it is certainly impossible to change our heredity, our genetic coding, or our parents.

We need to not only find the causes of our psychological blocks, we need to understand these causes in a way that will enable us to do something about them. So I propose this theory, and I encourage you to live and work with it a bit, and see if it doesn't do something useful for you: *the causes of our psychological blocks are the particular core beliefs that each of us has formed about ourselves, other people, and our world.*

This is not a new concept; there are several good books available on the subject.[2] But it is a crucially important concept, one which bears repeating until we fully grasp it and all of its ramifications, for it is a concept which, once we understand it and work with it, can and will change our lives and our world for the better.

"Core beliefs" are *the ideas and attitudes we have accepted as truth, either consciously or unconsciously.* Ever since earliest childhood, we have learned to accept things as being true or false in our world. Many of these things were oft-repeated words from Mommy or Daddy: we were good little kids, or bad kids, or bright, or stupid, or sloppy, or silly, or pretty, or dirty, and so forth. Many of these beliefs were things our brothers and sisters and peers told us, and we accepted them, often unconsciously. And, as children, all too many of us accepted a lot of negative beliefs, simply because kids tend to be so hard on each other, and on themselves. Kids learn to be highly competitive, because they are growing up in what appears to be a highly competitive world. Rarely does a kid consistently feel like a winner. So from a very early age, almost all of us developed some deep feelings of inadequacy. Teachers and the school systems have usually added a lot to our negative core beliefs, as well as highly competitive sports, grading systems, and even such accepted practices as IQ tests. Very few students come out of an IQ test feeling like a winner (and we can *all* become winners, once we understand the power of our core beliefs and our own thought processes).

Regardless of our past experiences, we have all created a great many core beliefs, some good, some bad, some that conflict with each other. We have accepted these core beliefs as truth, usually on a subconscious level. And, amazingly, every day we see confirmations of the truth of our beliefs. In fact, the world and everyone in it seems to act in accordance with our beliefs.

Most of the time we accept our core beliefs without examining them consciously. Many of them are harmful and negative, and many are contradictory, and cause confusion. Here are some typical negative core beliefs, expressed in the simplest possible language (the most effective way to express these beliefs, since many were developed in childhood):

> *I'm inadequate; I'm not complete in some way; I need someone else or something else to be happy; I'll never succeed; it's impossible to make enough money these days; the world is a dangerous place; my parents didn't raise me right; I had a deprived childhood; deep down, I can't really love anyone; I don't really have any good friends; I'm not okay; there's something wrong with me; I'm unworthy and undeserving; people (including me) are basically bad — selfish, cruel, stupid, untrustworthy, etc.; there's not enough (love, money, good things, etc.) to go around, so I have to struggle to get my share; it's hopeless, I'll never get enough, or if I have a lot, someone else will have to do without; love is dangerous — I might get hurt, or hurt someone; money is the root of all evil; money corrupts; the rich get richer and the poor get poorer; the world doesn't work and never will — in fact, it's getting worse all the time.[3]*

As you read through these negative ideas, see whether any of them reflect an underlying assumption of your own belief system. If so, you've taken the first step toward changing that belief, for *once you have consciously identified a core belief, you can begin to consciously change it.* For core beliefs aren't necessarily true in themselves. No core belief is true or false; only our thinking makes it so.

This makes even more sense in light of the widely varying beliefs that different people have about the same things. For example, a local magazine recently ran an article about the 100 most eligible women in the city. (This was followed by another article on the 100 most eligible men — both issues were very popular.) The article consisted of short interviews with many of the women, and two quotes from those interviews were boldly displayed to grab the reader's attention. One quote said that it was impossible to meet eligible men in this town, while the other claimed, "Everywhere I turn, I run into eligible men. They're all over the city." Though they were talking about the same city, they were obviously two different women with very different core beliefs.

Perhaps you have difficulty meeting people, or sustaining satisfying relationships with the people you meet. You have a great many reasons for this, of course, developed over a lifetime, and these are the reasons that support your core beliefs. You may feel your parents had a terrible relationship, or you had a horrible childhood. Maybe you were mistreated, isolated, or physically or psychologically damaged. Anyone of us who is not succeeding at something has reasons for justifying our lack of success, and our reasons are valid, because they are obviously true for us in the present.

Now, take a moment to absorb this: it doesn't matter what has happened to you in the past — the only thing that matters to you *now* is the particular set of core beliefs you have developed and are now carrying around with you, because those beliefs influence your behavior and your basic experience of life.

Core beliefs are self-fulfilling prophesies. If you believe you can't sing, for example, you certainly can't do it, and if you try to do it, you only work against yourself, and ultimately fail. This failure, in turn, becomes another reason to support your initial core belief that you really can't sing at all.

Changing Core Beliefs

How can we change core beliefs? It's quite simple, surprisingly simple for those of us who think any process of change has to be difficult, complex, mysterious, or painful. First, you have to accurately identify the core belief in the simplest possible words. Then you can gradually discard it, by repeatedly negating it verbally and emotionally and replacing it, repeatedly, with a new — and even more accurate — belief that works better for you. (This new belief is an *affirmation,* which we'll explore in detail in a moment.) After repeating this process, as often and as many times as necessary, your core belief will change for the better. This change will reflect the new conditioning you're giving yourself rather than the old negative conditioning. You'll know the core belief has definitely changed when your experience of the world definitely changes.

The next time you tell yourself that it's hard to find the right lover or that there's a scarcity of good people in the world, the next time you find yourself dwelling on what you don't have and affirming to yourself that you can't have what you want, drop the word "can't" from your vocabulary, and start telling yourself you *can* have what you want. Tell yourself repeatedly, until you thoroughly convince yourself not only consciously, but subconsciously as well.

The Core Belief Process

It's not always easy to discover core beliefs and express them in a simple, brief sentence that gets to the heart of the problems we're creating for ourselves. Core beliefs can be elusive, especially for those of us who tend to intellectualize a great deal — the "rampant rational mind" type — or for those who tend to become engulfed in overwhelming emotions — the "rampant emotional" type. while there is certainly nothing wrong with either our rational minds or our emotions, the two need to be balanced, in harmony. When one quality begins to dominate the other, we lose touch with our natural, innate clarity, and create far more problems for ourselves than necessary.

When we are emotionally upset, it is especially difficult for us to identify the core belief that is operating. We have developed a process, called the "core belief process," which is especially designed to identify these beliefs in the midst of an emotional problem, or following an emotional event that remains unresolved.

The process can be done either with a partner or alone. If done with a partner, one of you should ask the questions while the other answers, taking just a few minutes for each question. If you do it alone, you can write your answers to each question, or just answer them silently to yourself, or speak into a tape recorder and replay the tape afterwards.[4]

To begin, sit silently for a moment, eyes closed.

Take a deep breath, and relax as you exhale. Then think of the particular situation, problem, or area of your life you want to improve.

Now proceed through the following steps:

1. Describe the nature of the problem, situation, or area of your life you want to work on. Take about three or four minutes to talk about it generally.

2. What emotions are you feeling? Name the specific emotion, i.e., fear, sadness, anger, guilt. (Do not describe the thoughts you are having about it, at this point.)

3. What physical sensations are you feeling?

4. What are you thinking about it? (What 'conditioning' or "programming" can you identify? What negative thoughts, fears, or worries are you having?) Take a few minutes to describe your thoughts.

5. What is the worst thing that could happen in this situation? (What is your greatest fear?) If that happened, then what would be the worst thing that could happen? What if that happened? Then what would be the very worst thing that could possibly happen?

6. What is the best that could possibly happen? Describe the way you would ideally like it to be, your "ideal scene" for this area of your life.

7. What fear or negative belief is keeping you from creating what you want in this situation? Once you have explored this question, write your negative belief in one sentence, as simply and precisely as you can. If you have more than one, write down each of them.

8. Create an affirmation to counteract and correct the negative belief. We will talk about affirmations in the next section, but for now, here are some guidelines:

(a) The affirmation should be short, as simple as possible, and meaningful for you. Example: "I am a worthy person. I deserve to be loved!"

(b) It should be in the present tense, as if it is already happening. Example: "I now have a loving relationship."

(c) The affirmation should directly relate to your basic negative belief and turn it into a positive, expansive one. Some examples follow:

Negative belief: "I'm unattractive and unloving."

Affirmation: "I am attractive and loving!"

Negative belief: "I'm under a lot of stress at work, and it's unavoidable in my high-pressure job."

Affirmation: "I now relax and enjoy myself at work, and accomplish everything easily, effortlessly, and successfully."

(d) Your affirmation should feel exactly right for you. It should cause a strong, positive emotional feeling. If it doesn't feel right, keep changing it until it does.

9. Say or write your affirmation repeatedly:

(a) Repeat your affirmation silently to yourself, while relaxing, picturing everything working out exactly as you want it.

(b) Write your affirmation 10 or 20 times a day, until you feel you have absorbed it as a positive core belief. If negative thoughts arise as you are writing your affirmations, write your negative thoughts of the paper, then keep writing the affirmation on the front until it feels clear.

That's the entire core belief process. I've seen it have a very profound, positive effect on a great many people, including myself. All you need is the willingness to be honest with yourself. Your spontaneous answers to these questions may surprise you. After doing the affirmations, a lot of people, myself included, have felt a wave of relief, a feeling that can only be described as feeling a lot *lighter.* It is as if we were carrying around an emotional weight on our shoulders, which in many cases we weren't even fully aware of, and we've suddenly let it go. The result can be exhilarating. Try it and see.

The Power of Affirmations and Visualization

As you do the core belief process, you will discover that the right affirmation can have a deep, positive effect on you. In fact, it can change your life. *Affirmations are the single most powerful tool we have for creating and sustaining the relationships we want, for affirmations can literally restructure our negative core beliefs.*

Some explanation may be necessary to help you understand how this works, especially if you're naturally skeptical. As I've said before, I'm not asking you to believe this, but to accept the possibility and, with an open mind, try it out for yourself. To some people, the words 'affirmation' and 'visualization' themselves are difficult to relate to, suggesting difficult or esoteric processes. Actually, there's nothing difficult or esoteric about affirmation and visualization; in fact, they are simply two very natural processes which we are doing all the time, sometimes consciously, usually unconsciously.

The word affirmation comes from the Latin word *affirmare*, and it literally means "to make firm." Affirmations do indeed "make firm;" they literally create the reality we desire. How can this be so?

We are naturally creative beings. In the broadest, deepest sense, we have all created our present life situation. We have created our own experience of reality, although in most cases, not consciously but subconsciously. We have created the life situations that we feel, in some way, we deserve. In other words, the core beliefs we have accepted about ourselves have led us to subconsciously create the life we're now living.

How do we create something, anything? How do we write a book or knit a sweater, how do we repair a leaky sink or buy livingroom furniture? First, we develop an intention to do something; that is, we *affirm* to ourselves that we're going to do it. "I'm going to write a book... I think I'll knit a sweater... I've got to repair that leaky faucet... we need some new livingroom furniture...." These are all affirmations, words that make firm your intention to do something.

Once the intention is firm, you summon the creative power of your mind (usually unconsciously, because we do it so often that the process is automatic) and visualize the results. Both our conscious, linear, verbal mind (usually associated with the left hemisphere of the cerebral cortex) and our so-called "subconscious" or intuitive, spontaneous mind (usually associated with the right hemisphere) have the power to visualize results. (There has recently been a great deal written about this.[5]) When visualization is done repeatedly, and when it is supported by our mental and physical energy, we actually create what we are affirming and visualizing.

Note that the word "visualizing" does not necessarily mean literally "seeing" the final results in actual form, although this is sometimes what happens, in our "mind's eye." Visualizing is often done in a nonvisual form, a form that can only be described as a knowingness or a certainty. For example, when you say, "I'm going to the store to get some milk and cookies," this simple statement involves both an affirmation and a visualization: you "see" yourself going to the store — or you know or are certain you will — and you affirm that you will do so by your statement, whether it's spoken out loud or just a thought in your mind. Your affirmation and visualization direct your physical energy, and you end up creating your desired reality, in this case, milk and cookies.

We are constantly visualizing and affirming, but we usually do it unconsciously, and in a way that too often creates negative results. To become clearly aware of this critically important problem, try, for *one hour*, to be fully aware of everything you are affirming to yourself in both your spoken words and unspoken thoughts. This "meditation in action" is a surprisingly difficult exercise, but even a few minutes of effort can be an enlightening experience. No wonder we create things we don't really want in our lives, no wonder we can't get what we want. No wonder the world is in such a precarious mess! Look closely at your own words and thoughts, and multiply them by four billion!

Many of our words and thoughts reflect the core beliefs we developed at very early ages: I can't do this, I'm incapable, this is too hard for me to handle, I don't know how, , I'm unattractive, and so on. Even more of our core beliefs, however, are a recent development, a result of the nearly constant barrage of negativity from the media and from other people: the world's a mess, taxes are too high, it's so hard to succeed in today's world, it's so hard to find the right person, I need something else to make me attractive, and many, many other negative statements.

It's unfortunate, but these ideas, whether spoken out loud or whether they are deep, hardly noticed recurrent thoughts, are powerful affirmations that create the reality we are affirming.

On the other hand, *fortunately*, it's not that difficult to overcome even a lifetime of negative self-conditioning. All it takes is the desire to change, perseverance, and an understanding of the process. When you find yourself thinking negative thoughts, or saying negative things, replace those old words with new, positive words. Start seeing yourself as loving and capable, surrounded by a great many fine possibilities. Create positive, supportive core beliefs to replace the old, worn-out ones, and make your life much more enjoyable. You will probably be very surprised at how soon positive results will appear in your life.

As Richard Bach wrote,[6] "Argue for your limitations and they are yours." How true! Focus on your strengths instead, and they become even stronger.

Try the following affirmation on for size, and see how it feels. It is from the 100-year-old classic by James Allen, *As a Man Thinketh:*

You will become as great as your dominant aspiration.... If you cherish a vision, a lofty ideal in your heart, you will realize it.

As I write this, that quote is on my wall, right in front of me, written in large, bold letters. It is a constant reminder, a powerful, self-fulfilling affirmation. How much better to let words like these guide your life, rather than words of limitation. You can do what you want in life — all you need is the key that will unlock your own "vision and lofty ideals." That key is your power to affirm and visualize, a power you have always had but have not yet learned to use as skillfully, as effectively as you can.

An Exercise in Visualization and Affirmation

I suggested earlier that you take a few minutes and try to observe the negative affirmations you're creating, as they arise, and consciously change them to more positive affirmations that will create your desired reality. For example, suppose you find yourself thinking, "It's really difficult to find someone I'm compatible with for a long-term relationship." *As soon as you become aware of that thought in your mind,* firmly tell yourself, "I can easily find someone I'm compatible with!" Or if you find yourself thinking, "My boss is a pain in the neck," replace it with "My boss is a fine person," or even "My boss is a perfect expression of God, like everyone else," or whatever works for you. Do it firmly and quickly, before you find yourself getting that pain in the neck, or creating something even worse for yourself.

Always find an affirmation that feels good to you. Try different affirmations, if necessary, until you find one that is both positive and resonant for you personally. Otherwise, it won't be nearly as effective as it could be.

In addition to this kind of conditioning, I highly recommend the following short exercise. It requires only a few minutes a day (five minutes is adequate), four or five days a week, to create positive results in just a few weeks.

During these few minutes, relax, suspend all of your critical, rational, or "realistic" beliefs, and picture your *ideal scene*, affirming that you already have it. Although the following example focuses on creating the relationship you want, this simple exercise can be used to create *anything* you desire: health, wealth, wisdom, happiness, a peaceful environment, a new car, a good grade on a test, the solution to a problem, whatever. Try it and see.

> *Sit, or lie down comfortably. Close your eyes. Take a few deep breaths, and relax thoroughly... relax your body... relax your mind...let everything go — all worry, all thought, all doubts....As you relax, enjoy the feeling of simply breathing, simply relaxing.*

> *Now picture, as clearly and in as detailed a manner as you can, that which you want to create. Imagine it as if you have already created it, and are enjoying it.*

> *In this example, you will imagine the relationship you want with your ideal lover. Picture him or her, as clearly as you can. Picture the two of you together, surrounded by wonderful feelings of love. Spend a minute or two focusing on this, enjoying the imaginary scene you are creating.*

> *Then, find affirmations that nourish and support your visualization, and repeat them to yourself, over and over. Some examples for this exercise might be: "I now have a wonderful relationship with a loving*

*person." "I am now finding the perfect companion
for me." "The more I love, the more I am loved." "I
am now living with my ideal soulmate, who is ador-
ing and adorable." "I am now being guided into my
true place, and into the right relationship for me."
"So be it — so it is!" Use any words that work for
you.*

*Take a moment to enjoy and fully savor this
"fantasy" you have created. Add a few lovely details,
such as exchanging special, meaningful gifts, or doing
something you truly love to do. Play with your visualization, as if it already fully exists in the so-called
"real world."*

*Finish by taking one more deep, relaxing breath
and affirm to yourself, "This, or something better, is
now manifesting for the highest good of all concerned.
So be it — so it is!" (Put this very important final
thought in your own words.)*

*Open your eyes and come back to the "real world,"
feeling refreshed and relaxed, feeling the happiness
and contentment that comes with achieving what your
heart desires.*

Repeat the above exercise, focusing on the same thing,
four or five times a week. Soon — usually within two or
three weeks — you will absorb your visualization so
deeply into your subconscious that you will begin to see
results.

If the desired results don't manifest in a reasonable
amount of time, chances are that you're blocking yourself
in some way. Go back to the "core belief process" and
find out what core beliefs are preventing you from getting
what you want, and *deserve*, in your life.

If you are regularly visualizing and doing the core belief process, and *still* not getting what you want, you are probably making the common mistake of trying for too much too soon. While visualization and affirmation work for both short- and long-term goals, we can't expect long-term goals to manifest in a short amount of time.

Make your short-term goals — those things you can expect to accomplish in about six months or less — realistic. Total world peace is, unfortunately, not a realistic short-term goal at the present time. But the peaceful solution to specific problems may be. Finding the perfect partner and creating the perfect marriage may be too ambitious for a short-term goal, but meeting a wonderful person is certainly an excellent short-term goal.

On the other hand, make your long-term goals as idealistic and expansive as possible. This inspires you to stretch farther toward your greatest potential. Total world peace *is* an achievable long-term goal, as is your completely satisfying long-term relationship. You can develop all the long-term goals you wish, and then break them down into achievable, short-term steps. Take one step at a time up the ladder, using visualization, affirmation, and, if necessary, the core belief process, and before too long, you will be at the top.

This technique of conscious visualization and affirmation is very simple, it is true, and may seem too simple to those of us who feel that it should be somehow more complex in order to be effective. But you really *don't* need cassette or video tapes, biofeedback machines, submersion tanks, beads, mantras, gurus, or anything else to assist you in learning to use your own natural power of visualization and affirmation. You simply need to become aware of what you are thinking and what you are picturing for yourself. By consciously taking the time to imagine and affirm what you want in your life, you open the gates to the boundless power of your creative imagination. I have found this to be true in my own experience, and I challenge you to try some similar experimenting on yourself.

The Simple Act of Declaring

There is another, even simpler technique that involves no relaxation or examination of thoughts. We call it "declaring," from the Latin root, *declarare*, meaning "to make clear." By declaring, we are making it very clear to our powerful, creative mind exactly what we want.

Politicians and religious leaders often use declarations. Indeed, our country was founded with the *Declaration* of Independence — written, as you may remember, years before it was actually true in reality. Perhaps the greatest teacher of declarations was Christ, who said, "Ask, and you shall receive." Think about that one awhile, and take it to heart: ask and you shall receive! That's quite a declaration; it implies that if you haven't received what you want, you haven't clearly asked for it!

Here is a personal story that demonstrates the power of declarations. At one memorable point in my life, many years ago, I was ready for a change. For many reasons, I had come to feel that the primary relationship I had at that time was not going to work as a long-term relationship. My partner and I did a lot of honest soul-searching, both individually and with each other, and we came to realize that we couldn't stay together and still achieve what each of us wanted and needed in life. We ended the relationship (at least the intimate part of it) not bitterly, but sadly. We still had warm feelings for each other, and loved and respected one another. We wanted to continue as friends — which we still are, and always will be.

A few nights later, I found myself pacing the floor, asking myself a lot of questions. What did I really want? Did I want a committed relationship, or was it necessary for me to remain single in order to achieve my long-term career goals of living solely as a writer and composer? I examined the core belief I had developed, and realized that I had come to believe it was very difficult to survive in the precarious occupations of writing books and music and still have enough time, money, and love for a long-term, committed relationship. I saw that this belief was based on very limited thinking and I realized that *I didn't have to limit myself in any way.* I can do it, be it, and have it all; if I ask, I'll receive. I pictured what I really wanted, knowing I didn't have to accept anything less than that.

Without even consciously planning it, I stopped, spread out my arms, and declared out loud to the world (in the privacy of my livingroom), "I am ready to fall in love! I am ready to meet the *ideal* woman for me!"

I just declared these words one time, although I backed them up with a few sessions of visualization and affirmation, as I've described above. Just a few days later, I met her. And we've been together ever since.

To discover the power of declaration for yourself, state confidently to yourself that you are ready for the relationship you want and deserve. As it is said in the *Bible*[7],

> *And you shall declare a thing, and it will be given unto you....*

Try it and see for yourself.

Taking Action

There is a final step involved in creating what you want in life. It is obvious to most of us, but those who make the same affirmations *for years* and never seem to get any results are probably overlooking it. The step is taking action in the world and carrying out your creative ideas.

Although I have repeatedly seen that many things we visualize and affirm simply manifest, with little or no effort beyond the visualizing process, in most cases some form of action is necessary. Usually, after visualizing something for a while, we'll get some creative idea, such as an impulse to go somewhere, or get in touch with someone, or do something that ultimately leads us to the fulfillment of our desires. I am visualizing and affirming the completion of this book, for example, but I am also scheduling several mornings a week to sit down and write it.

It is certainly true that "God helps those who help themselves." How could it be otherwise? It is not even necessary to believe in a "God" as such to see the truth in this old saying; you can define "God" as anything you wish, such as your natural, innate power of creation: a power we all have and exercise daily, for better or for worse. Your natural power of creation is at your fingertips, within your creative mind.

Five Steps to Fulfillment

We're ready now to summarize what we have discussed so far with "Five Steps to Fulfillment." You can take these steps to fulfill anything your heart desires, from a wonderful lover to world peace, from a new car to financial independence.

Each step is necessary; if any step is left out, the results (with a few exceptions) will either not come at all, or they will be disappointing.

(1) Accept the situation as it is, for the present. Trying to force change out of frustration or anger usually creates more problems than it solves. Start by accepting things as they are. This does not mean that things will remain this way. It only means that you need to let go of resentment and anger over the past events which created the present situation. It is much easier to create a desirable future if you let go of negative feelings about the past and present and start fresh, accepting what has been and what is in current reality.

(2) Focus on what you want. As simple as this sounds, it is something most of us neglect to do in our lives. Before you can have what you want, you must become very clear about exactly *what* you want. Take the time to do some honest soul-searching before you try to create what you want. Make sure you *really* want it, and are prepared to deal with the consequences of having it. Make sure that it is "in alignment" with your goals and purposes in your life (more on alignment later).

(3) Eliminate personal blocks. Examine your core beliefs carefully to discover where you are limiting yourself and blocking yourself from creating what you want in life. Do the core belief process, either formally or informally, until these blocks have been dissolved.

(4) Affirm and visualize your results. Do a short exercise in the morning and/or evening, picturing the results you want and affirming to yourself that you *already* have what you want. During the day, keep repeating the affirmation, especially when and if you find yourself thinking negative or limiting thoughts, or in some way denying what you want to achieve.

(5) Take action. Back up your creative ideas with your time and energy. Follow up your impulses with action. Schedule specific times if necessary.

If you can take these five steps, you're ready to create what you want in life.

2

OBSTACLES TO SATISFYING RELATIONSHIPS

A particular train of thought persisted in, be it good or bad, cannot fail to produce its results on our character and circumstances. We cannot directly choose our circumstances, but we can choose our thoughts, and so indirectly, yet surely, shape our circumstances.

If you would protect your body, guard your mind. If you would renew your body, beautify your mind. Thoughts of malice, envy, disappointment, or despondency rob the body of its health and grace. A sour face does not come by chance; it is made by sour thoughts.[1]

—James Allen

WHAT ARE THE MAIN OBSTACLES we encounter as we try to create fulfilling relationships? They are all the numerous and varied mistakes we make in the course of trying to achieve what our hearts desire. But the mistakes themselves, in the long run, are not really the problem; the problem is how we react to our mistakes, how we deal with them when we make them. For, just as it is our nature as human beings to keep growing throughout our lives, it is also natural to make mistakes in the process. In fact, making mistakes is vitally important; they are essential to our learning and growth.

Our reactions to our mistakes, however, are not always conducive to our growth. Too much regret for our mistakes can prolong our suffering and cause us to mentally and emotionally "beat ourselves up." Some may even carry an emotional weight caused by the pain and regret of past mistakes for their entire lives. This burden prevents them from enjoying themselves and their lives, prevents them from making creative leaps, taking risks, and growing into more successful, fulfilled people.

The most effective way to deal with mistakes is to accept them and then let them go, focusing on *what you have learned* from those mistakes rather than the mistakes themselves. You have made a mistake for a reason: you did not know any better at the time. Now, having made the mistake and suffered for it in some way, you can learn from it and take steps to make sure that you won't make the same mistake twice.

So, instead of feeling guilty or putting yourself down when you make mistakes, rather than allowing them to limit you, turn your mistakes into valuable lessons which teach you to be a better person and to lead a more enjoyable and worthwhile life. Learning from our mistakes enables us to create more satisfying relationships with others.

The first step in profiting from our mistakes is to acknowledge them. As we saw in the core belief process, it often is helpful to be as honest as possible in evaluating our actions. The following checklist will help you to assess your own traits, traits that can destroy a perfectly good relationship if you allow them to. As you consider each statement, mark it true or false in the book or on a separate piece of paper. Be as honest as you possibly can. Try to remember any relevant comments from friends and lovers as you go through this list: we see other people's shortcomings so clearly, and yet we are so often blind to our own, so comments from others can help you evaluate yourself more clearly. Are you falling for any of these traps, even in some minor ways? It takes total honesty with ourselves, and it takes the willingness to be able to listen to what others are telling us, without denying what they are saying, defending ourselves, or putting ourselves down in some way.

The Critic

☐ True ☐ False   1. I am often critical of my lover.

☐ True ☐ False   2. I am often critical of others.

☐ True ☐ False   3. I often focus on what is wrong with social situations, my work situation, and so forth.

☐ True ☐ False   4. I feel my lover needs to change in order for our relationship to work.

☐ True ☐ False   5. I feel my lover is far less capable than I am in many areas.

☐ True ☐ False   6. I have more to offer my lover than my lover is able to offer me.

☐ True ☐ False   7. My lover has some serious shortcomings that need improvement.

☐ True ☐ False   8. I resent things my lover has done in the past which have hurt me.

☐ True ☐ False   9. I resent things my lover did before we met.

☐ True ☐ False   10. Sometimes my lover is really quite stupid or "unconscious."

☐ True ☐ False   11. My lover was not brought up well.

☐ True ☐ False   12. My lover's parents are really inept in some ways.

☐ True ☐ False   13. I resent the way my parents brought me up.

☐ True ☐ False   14. I rarely acknowledge my lover's good qualities.

The Paranoid or Pessimist

☐ True ☐ False   1. I worry about how things are going to work out in the future.

☐ True ☐ False   2. I keep imagining the worst is going to happen.

☐ True ☐ False   3. I have a basically pessimistic outlook.

☐ True ☐ False   4. I often forget to acknowledge the pleasant things I experience in life.

☐ True ☐ False   5. I worry that my lover will leave me.

☐ True ☐ False   6. The world, including my family, doesn't treat me right.

☐ True ☐ False   7. The world is a dangerous place.

☐ True ☐ False   8. Something else would be so much better than what I've got, but I'll never be able to achieve it.

☐ True ☐ False   9. I'm never going to get what I want in life.

☐ True ☐ False   10. Other people are to blame for my status and situation in life.

☐ True ☐ False   11. The world is basically a fearful place.

The Controller

☐ True ☐ False   1. I'm the only one who really knows what is best for my lover and my family.

☐ True ☐ False   2. In most situations, I feel I must have my own way.

☐ True ☐ False   3. I often try to control situations.

☐ True ☐ False   4. I feel I have to direct the show, because I'm really the only one capable of doing it.

☐ True ☐ False   5. Most people are basically either destructive or gullable, and they *need* to be controlled.

☐ True ☐ False   6. Sometimes I have to manipulate people for their own good.

☐ True ☐ False   7. I find that I manipulate people by withholding my love and appreciation until they do something I want them to do.

☐ True ☐ False   8. I'm actually quite good at getting other people to do what I want.

☐ True ☐ False   9. If it weren't for me, my whole family would just fall apart.

☐ True ☐ False   10. I can sense people's weaknesses and vulnerability and I use them to my best advantage.

The Time-Mismanagement Specialist

☐ True ☐ False   1. I rarely have any time for myself.

☐ True ☐ False   2. I rarely share "quality time" with my lover.

☐ True ☐ False   3. I'm basically a workaholic.

☐ True ☐ False   4. There's never enough time to do everything I have to do.

☐ True ☐ False   5. I'm always running behind schedule.

☐ True ☐ False   6. I never get enough done.

☐ True ☐ False   7. It's very difficult for me to just relax at home.

☐ True ☐ False   8. It's difficult for me to relax anywhere.

☐ True ☐ False   9. Other people make far too many demands on my time.

Liar and Cheater

☐ True ☐ False   1. I feel I'm a pretty good liar.

☐ True ☐ False   2. There are certain situations in which I can't possibly tell the truth.

☐ True ☐ False   3. I cheat on my lover and don't tell.

☐ True ☐ False   4. I sometimes feel guilty for lying to my lover.

☐ True ☐ False   5. I sometimes feel guilty for cheating on my lover.

☐ True ☐ False   6. I have gotten angry at my lover for asking questions.

☐ True ☐ False   7. If my lover would give me what I want, I wouldn't have to lie or cheat.

The Bore

☐ True ☐ False   1. I'm bored with my relationship.

☐ True ☐ False   2. My lover is a boring person.

☐ True ☐ False   3. I am a boring person.

☐ True ☐ False   4. I'm basically lazy.

□ True □ False   5. I don't really bother to take very good care of myself.

□ True □ False   6. My lover and I don't have a lot to say to each other anymore.

□ True □ False   7. We almost always eat dinner while watching television.

The Martyr

□ True □ False   1. I never do anything for myself — it's always for someone else.

□ True □ False   2. I'm always doing things for my lover and/or my children, but they rarely do things for me.

□ True □ False   3. I tell my lover (and/or my children) that I'm doing it all for them.

□ True □ False   4. I had dreams, I had potential, but I had to give them up for my lover and/or my kids.

□ True □ False   5. I've had to make a lot of sacrifices in my life.

□ True □ False   6. I suffer physically.

□ True □ False   7. I suffer emotionally.

□ True □ False   8. I suffer mentally.

Dominant/Submissive

☐ True ☐ False   1. One of us is quite intelligent, and the other is quite stupid.

☐ True ☐ False   2. One of us has it together; the other just can't cope without being told what to do all the time.

☐ True ☐ False   3. One of us definitely "wears the pants" in the family.

☐ True ☐ False   4. One of us never listens to the other.

☐ True ☐ False   5. One of us makes all the important decisions.

☐ True ☐ False   6. One of us is basically dominant, and the other basically submissive.

The Existentialist

☐ True ☐ False   1. I act on my impulses, and live to regret it.

☐ True ☐ False   2. I've walked away from relationships in the past and now I regret it.

☐ True ☐ False   3. It doesn't really matter whether or not I ever have a successful relationship in my life.

☐ True ☐ False   4. It's so hard to have a successful relationship, nearly impossible, in fact.

☐ True ☐ False   5. I find that I don't try very hard; it would eventually lead only to heartbreak for one or both of us anyway.

☐ True ☐ False   6. Deep down, I'm incapable of loving anyone else.

☐ True ☐ False   7. I don't really like myself very much.

☐ True ☐ False   8. I'm not capable of building a sustained relationship.

☐ True ☐ False   9. Living with another encroaches on my freedom.

☐ True ☐ False   10. I don't know what it means to love.

☐ True ☐ False   11. I've never been taught to love.

☐ True ☐ False   12. My parents had a loveless relationship.

☐ True ☐ False   13. Very few people I've ever known have had successful relationships.

☐ True ☐ False   14. I don't see what any sensible person would see in *me* as a lover.

☐ True ☐ False   15. Some of my lovers have complained that I am excessive with alcohol or other drugs.

Your Personal Inventory

As you go through the checklist, you will undoubt-edly find that some sections will have many more "True" markings than others. It is very important to spend some time working with these sections, because every answer marked "True" is a red flag, pointing to a core belief that needs some examination and work.

Every one of the "True" statements above can be positively changed by working with the core belief process. You don't *have* to play the role of the critic, the paranoid or pessimist, the controller, the time mismanagement specialist, the liar and cheater, the bore, the martyr, the dominant/sub-missive, or the existentialist. By working with the core belief process, and with the communication game we'll present later, you can create other, more successful role models for yourself. You can create successful, satisfying relationships.

3

OTHER ESSENTIAL STEPS

To desire is to obtain; to aspire is to achieve.... Dream lofty dreams, and as you dream, so shall you become. Your vision is the promise of what you shall one day be; your ideal is the prophecy of what you shall at last become.[1]

— James Allen

Defining Your Perfect Relationship

THE GREAT WRITER Goethe once wrote two short lines that contain a powerful, creative idea. I have this verse mounted on my desk, and I highly recommend copying it and putting it in a prominent place, so that it will eventually become etched in your mind:

Whatever you can do, or dream you can, begin it. Boldness has genius, power, and magic in it.

We've prepared ourselves psychologically, working with our core beliefs and examining patterns that have prevented us from achieving satisfying relationships in the past. Now we're ready to create the relationships we want. It is time to begin doing, being, and having what we want in life, time to take those bold steps that unlock our innate "genius, power, and magic": those natural forces of creation we all possess. All it takes is the willingness to take a risk, and the desire to pursue what we want. We'll certainly never regret trying.

The more clearly we define to ourselves exactly what we want, the better our chances are of achieving this goal. This seems like a simple, obvious statement, yet many of us never define our goals clearly, even though this is an essential step in achieving anything. The exercise in visualization and affirmation in Chapter One is an excellent method for helping you clearly see what you want. In doing this exercise, allow yourself the time to play with your imagination until you get a very specific picture of the relationship you want and the person you want to be with. What do they look like? What kind of person are they? How do they live? What kind of work do they do? What activities do you like to do together?

Be as specific as possible; this will not limit your choices because you can always revise your goals later. Visualizations can be easily adapted to any new circumstances you may encounter. For example, although you may have imagined meeting your perfect redhead, in actuality you might meet a black-haired someone who feels just right in all other respects. Suddenly, your ideal dream's hair has changed to black.

This applies to any goals you may have in life. Many of us are afraid to make specific goals, perhaps because we fear they will limit us in some way. Yet it's essential to define our goals in detail before we can actually take steps toward accomplishing these goals. The trick is to be precise, yet *flexible* enough to change our goals as often as necessary.

So take the necessary time, and dare to define your perfect relationship. Make sure you get exactly what you want; visualize your goal clearly in your mind's eye. If you can stay focused on that image, you're bound to create it, whether you know the steps you'll need to take, or whether you just happen to "stumble into it."

In a recent issue of *Money* magazine, there was a good example of a person who is clearly defining the relationship she wants. The article was about a young woman, a secretary in Minneapolis, who wants to marry a millionaire. Not just any millionaire, but someone who appeals to her heart as well as her bank account. Unlike those of us who have vague dreams or even clear goals that we are not pursuing actively, this woman has created a definite game plan for success, and is acting on it. She saves her money so she can eat lunch twice a week at one of the most exclusive restaurants in town, where millionaires usually dine. She joined a highly exclusive, and expensive, health club as well. When the article was written, two millionaires had already proposed to her, though she had turned them both down because they were not close enough to her ideal. With her determination and her clear visualization I have no doubt that she will soon meet with success — if she hasn't already.

If you define what you want and act on it, if you refuse to accept any belief that limits your dreams, you'll soon find yourself living the life you are dreaming of living.

Making Room in Your Life for Your Lover

Too many of us today have created a lifestyle that does not allow enough time for either ourselves or our lovers. This is a primary obstacle to having a successful relationship; we may not give enough time to the relationship, or we may destroy perfectly good relationships because we don't give enough time to *ourselves*. Managing a successful life is similar to managing a successful business: you've got to learn to budget your time to include your most important priorities. Since work expands to fill the time allotted to it, be sure to plan your time so that you have plenty of time for both yourself and your lover.

Make room in your life for your relationship, so you are sure to have time to be with your lover, to share the day's experiences, to enjoy each other. Just as importantly, make room in your life for yourself to do what you want to do. Don't ever get so busy that you don't have time to take a walk, or be alone with yourself when you need it. Taking time for yourself refreshes and rejuvenates you, so that you have much more to give to others.

Meeting Your Lover: the All-important First Moment

This section will be especially helpful to those who believe they have difficulty meeting potential lovers and friends. It has always surprised me that so many people have this difficulty, yet it is all too common. Many of us have developed the core belief that it is difficult to meet attractive, desirable people. Like any core belief, this is not necessarily true in itself, and it can be changed by working with the core belief process given earlier.

Perhaps I never developed negative core beliefs about the difficulty of meeting people, because I have always found it very easy and natural. This is probably something I learned from my father: he has been happily married for over 45 years and is certainly not looking for any other romantic relationships, but he has a relaxed, friendly openness with everyone he encounters, and he is always meeting and talking to new people. When he sits down at a bar for a drink, for example, he always says, "Hi, how are you doing?" to whoever is sitting next to him, whether they're young or old, male or female. His open friendliness almost always causes people to respond to him in a friendly way — and he is filled with stories of his many conversations with a great number of different, interesting people.

Because I was exposed to this natural openness as I was growing up, I now find it easy to meet people of all kinds. All that is necessary is to be friendly, spontaneous, and nonthreatening.

I've found that *the very first moment* is the most important moment when meeting someone, especially when you're casually meeting a stranger in a public place. For example, suppose a very attractive person walks up behind you in a line at the post office. That first moment is the best time for a smile and a friendly "Hello," which can easily lead to a casual conversation about the weather, the length of the line, something they're wearing — whatever pops into your mind. The longer you wait to say something, the more difficult it becomes to say anything at all, and the more stilted and forced it sounds when you try to initiate the conversation.

If you have trouble meeting people, try jumping into a conversation in that first spontaneous moment of contact with someone. The opportunity arises so often, especially in the cities, but too often people cut themselves off from meeting one another, through shyness or other fears.

Any time, anywhere, is the perfect time and place to meet people. Practice being open to others, saying "Hello" with a smile, or saying whatever comes to mind, in a friendly, nonconfrontive way. Don't be afraid to fail or make a fool of yourself; after all, it is much better to have tried and failed than never to have tried at all! Sooner or later, you're bound to connect with a very special person.

A special friend of mine has a sign over her front door that says, "There are no strangers — only friends we haven't met yet." If you start looking at your world this way, and try to avoid that all-too- common sense of isolation and separation, your world will become a much friendlier place. And you will easily meet as many people as you wish. After all, you have over four billion possible friends and lovers on this planet — that's certainly enough for all of us.

4

THE FINE ART OF COMMUNICATION

I give to you the best gift there can be
I give you a mirror and now you can see
The wonder you are! to see is to be free
Look in the mirror now miracles unfold
in front of thee[1]

A T SOME POINT in most of our lives, we create a romantic relationship we wish to sustain. This is not true for everyone; there are some who find living alone more fulfilling, and some who are genuinely more satisfied to live with others without sexual involvement. But most of us seek the stability and pleasure of a sustained intimate relationship.

If so many people want a sustained romantic relationship, why is there so much separation and divorce today? There is no single, simple answer, because there are a great many answers for a great many different people. One important reason is that most people haven't ever learned how to communicate effectively, how to express their feelings, whether they are feelings of anger, fear, love, or anything else.

There is another important reason: most people are no longer pressured by their families and society to continue in relationships that aren't working successfully. A generation ago, most people tended to stick with their marriage for life, whether they were happy with the relationship or not. Most of us probably know someone who does not seem to have a satisfying marriage, but keeps it together for the sake of the children, for financial reasons, or because they are afraid to be alone or are simply afraid of any change. But today, for many of us, these are not valid reasons for continuing an unhappy marriage. Today, there are a great number of alternatives available.

Yet it is sad to see so many potentially fine relationships fall apart, especially when many of them could be sustained if the people involved knew how to talk with each other in a way that would clear up resentment between them, and if they knew how to renew the basic, genuine feelings of love that brought them together in the first place. It's possible to learn these fine arts: all it takes is a bit of work, and a bit of understanding.

"Moral Freedom"

If your intimate relationship was worth creating in the first place, it is very likely that it is worth sustaining. Sometimes it isn't, but that decision is entirely yours to make. We are fortunate, I feel, to be living in a unique age: today we are free to make our own decisions and live the kind of life we want to, without having to submit to pressure from parents, peers, churches, and society in general. We may still face a lot of that pressure, depending on the choices we make for ourselves, but now they *are* our choices.

It has finally become socially acceptable, for instance, for a woman to live alone, with or without children. Or, a woman may live with other women and not feel an overwhelming pressure to get married, have children, and live in a house in the suburbs. In most parts of the country, a man and a woman may live together without making the commitment of marriage, though even a few years ago, this was completely unacceptable. This attitude does still exist in some areas of the country, but even these areas are changing, largely due to the growing number of people who no longer accept such standards.

Today, we do not have to accept discrimination or pressure from others who would attempt to force us to do something we don't really want to do. We finally have the freedom to live the way we truly want to live. The challenge today is to learn how to embrace that freedom.

Perhaps the words of Henry David Thoreau, written not too long after America's independence, are finally coming true:

> *Do we call this the land of the free? What is it to be free from King George and continue to be the slaves of King Prejudice? What is it to be born free and not to live free? What is the value of any political freedom, but as a means to moral freedom?...It is our children's children who may perchance be really free.*[2]

We may be the first generation in this country to actually attain a significant degree of "moral freedom": the opportunity to create our chosen lifestyle, to determine *for ourselves* how we live. At least this is true for many of us, if we have the strength and the desire to think and dream for ourselves. Throughout history, there have always been those who have attained this kind of freedom, although they often faced tremendous opposition for their views and their lifestyles. Fortunately, this kind of opposition is weakening today.

Two Keys to a Successful Relationship

In this part of the book we will focus on the fine art of sustaining a worthwhile relationship. Again, this is a subject you will rarely find taught in school. (Imagine courses such as "Creating Satisfying Relationships" or "Sustaining Intimate Relationships" being taught in high schools and colleges. Perhaps some of our more enlightened schools are already teaching courses such as these. They're vitally important subjects — and I'm sure they would be popular courses!)

The two most important keys to sustaining any relationship are: (1) developing effective communication, and (2) continuing to visualize the relationship as being deeply satisfying for both of you.

In this chapter, we'll discuss communication, a fine art which today seems to be nearly a lost art in most people's lives.

The Fine Art of Communication

Like any fine art, communication can be taught. Unfortunately, most of us have not been taught to communicate effectively, especially when we have something unpleasant to say, something we want to say when we're angry and upset, sad, worried, or depressed. It is difficult to express irritation with others so they will understand and not become upset and reject everything you say. A lot of people think it isn't even possible, and so don't even try, until their irritation develops into an overwhelming anger which bursts out at the wrong time and causes even more anger, hurt, and guilt. This often leads to separation of some kind, or even the end of the whole relationship. This is unfortunate, because if we take the time and trouble to learn how to talk to each other in a way that minimizes alienation, we can find ourselves coming even more closely together, discovering a new kind of love and appreciation, rather than drifting apart.

For all too many people, "communication" is merely a buzzword, a term that is no longer respected — or, worse yet, it is avoided entirely. This is sad, because good communication is one of the most powerful tools we have for creating and sustaining happy, healthy relationships.

Speaking Your Mind Freely

In any kind of relationship — whether it involves lovers, families, employers and co-workers, or even in international relations — *everyone involved has the right and must be given the opportunity to speak their minds freely* if the relationship is to work successfully. Everyone must have their say; otherwise, highly destructive feelings can develop. Ultimately, separation and even war can result when communication breaks down.

Most people need to learn how to communicate their honest feelings and offer their honest feedback without doing what we call "dumping" on others: without making other people feel as if they've been attacked, or suddenly inundated with someone else's built-up resentment, anger, and criticism. Tactful, successful communication is based on unconditional love, love given freely, not withheld until certain conditions are met. Helping your friends and lovers to honestly see themselves without creating a sense of separation takes gentleness and acceptance on your part.

Yet when problems arise, it's not always possible to be completely gentle and accepting, especially when you are feeling any of a number of feelings that have been called "separating" feelings: hurt, anger, jealousy, fear. When this happens, try the game that follows — *it may be the single most important thing you can do to sustain a fullfilling relationship.* For most people, the next two sections are by far the most important sections in this book.

An Example of the Communication Game

Before we list the six steps of the "Communication Game," it will undoubtedly be helpful to give you an example of how it can work in a real-life situation.

Sally and John live together. Lately, John has been going out drinking after work with increasing regularity. Sally is worried about him, and has become very critical of him and his apparent need to drink so much. One night he comes home looking somewhat drunk, feeling depressed and moody. They start to argue. Their argument rises in intensity until, as is usual with most arguments, they're interrupting each other continuously, and not listening to each other. They're both trying desperately to be heard, but without success. They are both angry and frustrated.

Finally, Sally says, "This is going nowhere. Let's try that 'argument-settling game' I read about the other day."

John resists: "I'm tired of playing games! I just want you to listen to me!"

Sally persists: "That's what the game is all about! What can it hurt to at least *try* it? It can't be worse than this!"

John finally agrees. (Note: he wouldn't even have to agree and Sally could still use the technique. We'll look at that later.)

They sit down, and Sally asks John if he wants to go first. John says that since Sally started the argument, she can go first. Sally begins by saying that, in her opinion, John started the argument. John starts to interrupt angrily, but Sally reminds him that he has to listen to her; he'll have his chance in a minute. Sally then tells John how much she is concerned about his drinking: she worries that he'll get stopped for drunk driving, she worries about his health, and she is resentful of the time he spends away from her while he's drinking. As she gets more involved in the process, she tells him, with feeling, that their relationship simply isn't working this way, with him coming home nearly drunk every night.

John becomes defensive and interrupts again, saying, "Not every night!"

Sally reminds John that he is interrupting her, *denying* what she is saying and *defending* himself. She reminds him that he is to simply listen without denying what she is saying, defending himself, or putting himself down.

She goes on to say that, regardless of what John feels, the drinking has become a big issue between them, and she doesn't want to continue the relationship in these circumstances. She feels she deserves something better, and wants to take some kind of action. She tells him that if he doesn't drink less, she'll leave him for good. It just isn't worth it to her to go on like this.

After a bit more of this, she feels complete. A lot of her anger has dissipated. She says, "Okay, now it's your turn." Sally's part of the process took less than five minutes.

John begins by defending his drinking. He realizes it's a defense, but it is what he feels: he doesn't *really* drink that much, at least not enough to affect his health, and he really enjoys it. Seeing an irritated, disgusted look on Sally's face, he says, "Look, you didn't interrupt me, but you're obviously denying what I'm saying. Can't you just sit there and listen to me without that expression on your face?" Sally apologizes, and makes an effort to simply listen without being too critical.

John goes on to say that he has been examining his reasons for drinking. He feels two things are bothering him that he hasn't really expressed clearly. One, he feels too pressured at work. He drinks coffee all day long and rushes around, never having enough time to do all that he needs to do. He is always behind schedule, is often criticized for it, and he feels frustrated by this. The drinking helps him relax and forget his work troubles. The other reason is that he feels there is a hopeless distance between the two of them. He feels she is too critical of him. He feels he does most of the work to support them both, at least he earns most of the money, and he is not appreciated for it. He feels he is working much harder than she is, at a much more demanding job. He realizes that he has built up quite a bit of resentment toward her because she is not contributing much money to their life together, yet she is highly critical of how he spends his money. It irritates him. And she's very happy to spend his money all too freely on what she wants. That irritates him too.

When John finishes, he finds he feels less angry. Sally then responds to John. She says she feels she contributes more to the relationship and works harder than he seems to realize. She, too, feels unappreciated for all the work she does and all the support she gives John. That's all she needs to say, this time, and this time John has no trouble letting her have her say without interrupting.

John responds again, acknowledging that he hasn't been very appreciative of her lately, but then he hasn't felt appreciated either. By now, both of them have cooled down quite a bit, because they've been able to express themselves in a way that makes them feel *they've been heard*. They haven't been interrupting each other, but rather waiting for the other to finish talking before they respond. They have actually, for the first time, been *listening* to each other, and they find themselves naturally becoming more sympathetic toward each other.

Sally then tells John what she wants from him. She wants him to drink less, first and foremost. She wants him to show more appreciation to her, to bring her a small gift occasionally, take her out more often, and simply tell her he appreciates her once in a while. She wants more affection, more loving.

Then John tells Sally what he wants from her. He, too, would like more appreciation for what he does. He wishes Sally would be more demonstrative of her affection; he too wants more closeness and loving. But he also wants time for himself, to do what he needs to do without feeling pressured to be with her, or to be doing something constructive around the house. He'd also like Sally to at least try to earn more money, to ease the financial pressure he feels.

They both realize they have calmed down, and they feel not only sympathetic, but even affectionate toward each other. Now they negotiate. John agrees to limit his drinking. He says he will make a rule to have no more than two beers a night — and no other type of alcohol — after work, before coming home. And he won't drink at all before coming home at least two days a week. He also agrees to take her out, at least once a week, like they did before they lived together. He ends by saying he really does appreciate all the things she does for him, and he will try to express his appreciation more often in the future.

Sally agrees to make every effort to give John the time he needs for himself. John says he would ideally like every Sunday to be totally free of commitments to Sally or anyone else, and Sally says she feels fine about that. Sally then says she realizes John has been carrying a big load financially, as business has slacked off considerably where she works, and her hours and paychecks have dwindled. She says she will start looking for a better-paying job.

After making these agreements, they both feel a lot better and much closer to each other. The entire session took less than twenty minutes. And they live happily together ever after (having more sessions like this occasionally, of course).

How to Settle an Argument: the Communication Game

The technique John and Sally used is a simple, six-step exercise or game that will help settle any argument. We call it the "communication game." One of the best things about it is that you can play it whether or not the other person is willing. But to explain the game clearly, I'll first assume there are two of you willing to play. Once you understand the rules, you will see how easy it is to use these techniques even on an unwilling partner. After all, both of you will win in the end, and that's the purpose of the game.

When you find yourself locked into an argument with someone, or when you have something to say to someone that has been bothering you, but you haven't dared to talk about it, go through the following six steps:

(1) *Stop arguing.* You can be sure the argument you're locked into is getting you nowhere. Refuse to continue arguing with the other person, even if the other person continues. Remember, it takes two to tangle — so just make the decision to stop arguing and abide by the rules of the game.

(2) *Allow your partner to completely express their feelings, without interruption, and without denying them, defending yourself, or putting yourself down as a result of what they're saying.*[3] Simply listen and accept what your partner is saying. This is usually the most difficult step, since it is especially difficult not to interrupt or react negatively, but it's the most important step, because it allows your partner to express their feelings without interruption. It also teaches you to absorb negative criticism without immediately reacting — an extremely valuable skill to gain.

(3) *Now it's your turn to express your feelings, as completely as possible,* and your partner must be quiet and listen. Encourage your partner, too, to hear what you're saying to them without denial or defense, or putting themselves down in any way.

Take as long as you need. In my experience with this technique, used many times over the years, it usually takes less than five minutes for each person to "blow off their steam" and express everything they have to say.

After the second person has finished, the first person will usually want to respond, and at this point, the second and third steps may be repeated once or twice (very rarely is it necessary to repeat them more often than this). Before long, you'll find the air clearing between you both. You'll realize how the continual interruptions of your earlier arguments fueled those arguments. When you stop interrupting each other and listen instead, the argument clears up. Now you can move on to the next step:

(4) *Ask your partner what they want from you,* providing the time and encouragement, without interruption, for them to tell you exactly what they want and need. Listen and remember. Every argument is based on the fact that the people involved aren't getting something they want. Then:

(5) *Tell your partner exactly what you want from them.* Now you're ready for the final step:

(6) *Negotiate with each other.* Make clear agreements with each other that work for both of you, just as John and Sally did. Compromise of some kind may be necessary for one or both of you, but keep negotiating until you reach an agreement that satisfies you both: a "win-win" agreement. It may require some time and some creative brainstorming to find something you both agree upon, but in almost every case you can find a creative solution that works for *both* of you.

Why the Communication Game Works

Why does this simple technique work so effectively? (Try it, and I know you'll agree.) There are at least two primary reasons, which I've hinted at before:

(1) When arguments start, we stop listening. Frus-

tration builds, and we say things that only make matters worse. As the argument builds in intensity, covert, cutting remarks become overt negative criticism. No one likes criticism; no one likes anger directed at them. The natural response is self-defense and anger. By playing the communication game, you get the satisfaction of having expressed your feelings in an environment where those feelings are heard. Frustration dissolves.

I once saw a graphic demonstration of the way frustration and anger literally dissolve when I played the game while connected to a galvanic skin-response machine. The meters registered my anger, and they dropped, slowly but steadily, as I expressed my feelings. The therapist called this "blowing off the charge." Before long, the meters registered a "flat" response: my anger had dissipated entirely.

(2) You can't get away with the all-too-common reactions of denial, defense, or putting yourself down. You are forced to listen, to accept and absorb what the other person is saying. In other words, you are forced into a mature response, one that teaches you to be more open to other people's opinions and feelings, and to grow as an individual. You don't necessarily have to believe what the other person is saying: you're completely free to ignore what you hear, if you feel that, for any reason, what they're saying is not appropriate for you. But you must at least hear what the other person is saying, and take a moment to consider it. In a surprisingly short time, this takes the steam out of every argument.

This technique can be used not only by close friends and lovers, but also by families, in classrooms, in offices and boardrooms, in shops and other work places, and even in conferences between nations. *It is possible for any problem to be solved in a way that everyone involved wins.* It may take quite a bit of time for negotiation, compromise, and creative thinking, but there is almost always a solution to be found which will work satisfactorily for everyone involved.

Once you understand how to use this technique, you can even use it effectively with people who don't know you're using it. If you find yourself in an argument, simply stop and say, "Look, this argument is getting us nowhere. I'm going to sit here and listen to everything you have to say, without interrupting you, and then I'm going to ask you to sit and listen to what I have to say, without interrupting me — okay?" They will almost always agree, because all they really want is to be heard.

Then let them have their say, let them release their pent-up frustration, without denying them, being defensive, or feeling sorry for yourself as a result of what they're saying. Don't interrupt — sometimes it seems to be the most difficult thing in the world, especially when you're burning to respond, but it is *essential* not to interrupt. Wait until they are finished. Then say, "All right — I listened to you. Now I'm asking you to listen to me, and not to interrupt until I'm finished."

In this way, you can take them through all the steps of the game, even if they would never have agreed to play it in the first place.

Nearly everyone can use some practice with this argument-resolving technique; nearly everyone can benefit from studying the fine art of communication.

The Importance of Feedback

When the "communication game" is played, you learn

another valuable lesson about the fine art of communication: the importance of the feedback you receive from others.

As you notice when you play the game, our natural tendency when confronted with something we don't like to hear is denial, self-defense, or putting ourselves down in some way. To simply allow ourselves to hear what others are saying, and absorb and consider it without denying it, seems very difficult at first.

If we can develop a new attitude about the feedback we receive from others, this open listening can become easy, and even enjoyable. The new, more mature (more *evolved*) attitude is this: *everything anyone says to us is useful for us in some way.* We may not like it, we may not agree with it, we may not even accept it (we certainly don't *have* to accept everything people say to us), but there is some useful information in everything everyone says to us.

Once you develop the core belief that you are basically a strong, worthwhile person, you find you feel confident and clear when relating to friends, relatives, lovers, anyone. You find you can listen to everything they have to say, accept the fact that they are speaking what they feel to be true, and usually discover something worthwhile in what they are saying. Although you may not agree, you can definitely be open to hearing what they have to say. This is the attitude of a powerful person, a person who is not threatened by others and doesn't have to deny, defend, or apologize.

Making Agreements and Commitments

The communication game also works because it inevitably leads to clear agreements and commitments. These are two of the most important features of all successful long-term relationships, yet few people recognize or consciously practice them. Some people are afraid of making agreements or commitments, or they are afraid of the word "negotiation," because it makes a romantic relationship feel like a business relationship. Yet, a romantic relationship does have a great many similarities to a business relationship; everyone involved needs to create a "win-win" situation, where they are all getting what they need from the relationship. This requires negotiation; it requires making agreements and commitments.

Look at our friends John and Sally: without the agreements they made at the end of the process, the same problems would continue to arise again and again. The communication game works beautifully for dissolving built-up resentment between people, but it requires subsequent *action*, in the form of clear agreements and commitments, to truly improve the relationship.

It is important that you and your friends and lovers only make agreements and commitments that *all of you* feel good about. This is where negotiation comes in. While Sally may have wanted John to quit drinking entirely, John may have felt that was too extreme, and proposed a limit of two beers per evening. Sally might then agree, providing the two beers are twelve ounces each, not quarts. If John feels fine about this, and so does Sally, then together they have both created a "win-win" situation.

In this example, the agreements concern a relatively specific issue, but agreements also need to be reached on the general form of your relationship and the direction in which you are both heading. The *form* of your relationship may be anything you both want, but it must be a form you both agree on and feel good about. Whenever problems arise between you, this friction is a sign that you need to make some kind of agreement. Don't hesitate to do so, because in the long run you both emerge as winners.

A Tip for Effective Communication

Often, in the busy course of our lives, things may occur — a brief comment, a momentary feeling — in a situation where it is impossible or undesirable to play the entire communication game. At these times, a very simple technique can get to the source of the problem quickly. It is so simple, yet so rarely done, that it may be startling when it is first done. All that is necessary is to ask the other person how they *feel* about whatever it is that is bothering them, and then give them time to express their feelings. Or, if it's something that has upset you, just say, "There's something bothering me about this..." and then go on and try to express your feelings as clearly as you can.

When problems arise, especially at work, most of us are involved primarily in mental activity, so we discuss the problem and try to "figure it out." By going directly to our emotional experience and expressing how we feel about a certain problem rather than dwelling on what we may think about it, we can learn a great deal and get to the root of the problem much more quickly.

When we focus on our feelings, our natural, intuitive instincts, we are led to more effective solutions than the endless process of rational thought can ever provide.

Getting into Alignment: Your "Ideal Scene"

Getting into alignment with your lover, your close friends and your co-workers is another important aspect of effective communication. Just as the tires on your car need to be in alignment so they won't wear out prematurely, lovers, friends, and co-workers need to be "in alignment," working toward similar goals. Relationships (and businesses) often run into difficulties because those involved aren't in agreement with each other about specific goals and more general life purposes. The need for agreement seems so obvious, yet how many couples honestly examine the compatibility of their goals, purposes, and dreams? This seldom happens because there is no framework in which to do it. To provide such a framework, I suggest the following game, called the "ideal scene."

> *Sit down with your lover or your business associates, and assume that five years have passed. During those five years, everything went as well as could possibly be expected for you. You are well on your way to achieving your "ideal scene" in life. In this future life, what are you doing? Where are you living? What is your typical day like? What kind of relationship do you have? Each player takes a turn describing this ideal scene, the more detailed, the better.*

This simple and enjoyable technique is very effective in clarifying long-range goals and plans. It tricks us into discovering something very important to every one of us: our goals in life, and even our greater *purposes* in life, something we rarely reflect on but feel deep within ourselves, whether we pay any attention or not. Of course, the more attention we pay to our goals and purposes, the more satisfied we will be with our life's experience.

Once you have talked through your "ideal scene" together, work on developing long-range plans that will help to satisfy *all* these needs and dreams, and start moving both of you toward your ideal. This exercise forces you to either come into alignment or to see that it is not possible for you to do so.

A marriage I knew of was typical of a lack of alignment. The couple loved each other deeply, and were very compatible living together in their daily life. Yet, what she really wanted was to live in the country and have horses, in or near her home state, Oregon. This was her dream, her long-range need, and it would have emerged had they played the "ideal scene" game together. While she wanted, more than anything, to raise and train horses, he was an actor and felt he needed to be in New York City or Los Angeles for a substantial period of time to achieve his goal. This was his dream, his long-range need. They moved to New York; she was very unhappy and their relationship suffered. When he decided to move to Los Angeles, she refused. They settled on San Francisco, because it was a compromise — halfway between Los Angeles and Oregon. But the compromise didn't really work for either of them.

Although they had a strong connection and both deeply wanted their marriage to succeed, they weren't in alignment about the life they both *needed* to live. Their relationship could only have continued if one of them was willing to compromise for a number of years, and support the other's goal. He felt a strong motivation to get his acting career moving, and she felt a strong resistance to living in Los Angeles or New York, even for a short period of time. He knew he couldn't ask her to just put up with it indefinitely because he honestly didn't know how long it would take, and didn't want to pressure himself into a deadline. They were deadlocked.

This lack of alignment destroyed an otherwise perfectly compatible relationship. Had they examined their "ideal scenes" before they made the commitment of marriage, separation would probably have been much easier. Their marriage finally did fall apart, and in the long run it was for the best. Each of them created another intimate relationship with someone more in alignment with their goals: he is with a woman who is also an aspiring actress, and he is doing very well in both his acting career and his relationship; his former wife is now with a writer who lives in northern California. She owns her own horse again, she is learning to train and show horses, and she is close to her friends and relatives in Oregon.

Living with a lover whose goals are not in alignment with your own can mean a life of frustration and emptiness, and can result in a great deal of covert (or even open) hostility, unhappiness, and possibly even physical illness or mental imbalance. Sometimes it is necessary to terminate a close relationship, even though it may have many good qualities, if you aren't getting what you need from it.

Take the time *now* to see if you are in alignment, or can get into alignment, in terms of your long-range goals and dreams.

Alignment in Business Relationships

"Getting into alignment" is as important in business as it is in personal life. In order for any business to be successful, there must be alignment from top to bottom. If you are involved in a partnership, it is *crucial* that the partners are in alignment, otherwise problems continually arise.

Areas that must be dealt with include not only financial considerations — who gets paid what, and how the money is spent — but also the type of workplace, the lifestyles of the people involved, the products or services the company produces, the direction of the company's growth, and its long-range plans for employees and directors.

When these factors are in alignment, success is almost certain.

How do you get into alignment in business? Do the "ideal scene" process together; give everyone involved a chance to express themselves, their goals, and their dreams. Then negotiate, working toward developing long-range plans that not only satisfy but challenge everyone as well. If there are problems, tensions that arise between people, have them play the communication game. *The effort you invest in getting into alignment is far more important than the effort you invest in your products and services.* If the people organizing and implementing the plans of the business aren't in alignment, it is very difficult to successfully market even the greatest products and services in the world.

Alignment Between Co-workers and Employers

It is essential to get into alignment with your co-workers and your employer, as well. Every business is really a single organism, with its own reason for being and its own life. Every person working for that business is there not only to earn a living, but to support everyone else as well. When co-workers and employers (we call them all "associates" in our business) clearly realize this, the business functions better. When tension, negative criticism, and unresolved emotions arise between anyone involved in the business, these things have to be dealt with in some kind of forum in order for the business to function smoothly.

Regular meetings can do wonders to clear the air, if everyone involved is encouraged to openly express their feelings, *especially* negative feelings. At our company, we have bi-weekly meetings that often begin or end with what we call a "clearing" session: everyone is encouraged to speak out if they feel tension, negative criticism, or unresolved emotions. After all, we're all in it together. Just publicly expressing such feelings can usually clear up the problems; sometimes negotiation may be necessary.

We also make it a rule to deal immediately with tensions or problems that arise during the day *only with the other person involved,* that is, with no one else present. If this is inconvenient, the discussion is delayed until it can be carried out in private. We also find it very helpful at times to play the communication game. Personal communication keeps the air clear, and the meetings keep us in alignment.

The bigger the business, the more difficult — and the more essential — it is to bring the various divisions into alignment within themselves and with each other. You know you have achieved alignment when everyone involved feels motivated to ensure that the business will succeed, and when every relationship within the business is a "win-win" relationship. This is a difficult challenge for a great many businesses, but it is certainly worth striving for.

5

KEEPING IT TOGETHER

The greatest achievement is at first and for a time a dream. The oak sleeps in the acorn; the bird waits in the egg; and in the highest vision of the soul a waking angel stirs. Dreams are the seedlings of realities.

Your circumstances may be uncongenial, but they shall not long remain so if you but perceive an ideal and strive to reach it. You cannot travel within and stand still without....Those who cherish a beautiful vision, a lofty ideal in their hearts, will one day realize it. [1]

—James Allen

PRACTICING THE FINE ART of communication is certainly one of the most essential ingredients in successful long-term relationships. Yet one more ingredient is even more essential. It, too, is a fine art.

The Fine Art of Visualization

The single most important element in both creating and sustaining a relationship involves the visualization of that relationship. This visualization is not to be taken lightly, it is not unimportant or insubstantial. *It is essential for success in anything.*

Before creating your visualization, ask yourself the following important questions, and take as much time as you need to answer these questions: What kind of relationship do you really want? What do you want your lover to be like? What kind of life do you want a few years from now? Five years from now?

Take your time; construct in your mind a clear picture of the kind of relationship you want. Guided by that clear picture, you will find the means necessary to achieve it. Over time, the necessary steps will become obvious. Be patient. This is not something that happens overnight.

As Rilke writes in *Letters to a Young Poet:*

> *I want to beg you, as much as I can, to be patient toward all that is unsolved in your heart; try to love the* questions themselves *like locked rooms or books that are written in a foreign tongue. Do not now seek the answers; they cannot be given to you now because you would not be able to live them. And the point is to live everything.* Live *the questions now. You will then gradually, without even noticing it perhaps, live along some day into the answer.*[2]

To ensure that the relationship you have created is successful, simply continue to visualize it as being deeply satisfying and fulfilling for both of you. I have repeatedly seen how problems dissolve in the light of a firm, clear visualization of success. And unfortunately, I have also seen problems multiply with the help of continual *negative* visualization, including fears that a relationship won't work out, worries that one or the other partner won't be satisfied in the long run, excessive jealousy, and many other anxieties such as these.

Our dominant visualizations are clearly visible in us, at a glance; they are expressed in our posture, facial expressions, and in the things we say. How many people do you know, for example, who can't even receive a compliment without in some way denying it or minimizing it? This is an unconscious attempt to deny the positive effect of the compliment, and so perpetuate a negative visualization. The next time you receive a compliment, pay close attention to what you feel and how you respond. The best response to a compliment is to thank the person and to affirm to yourself in some way that it is true. This accepts the power of the compliment, and uses it in a constructive way to actually increase your personal power.

As Neil Young sings in one of his songs, "Don't deny yourself."

Everything we say and do reflects our dominant visualizations and core beliefs. Pay attention to the things you say; they can teach you a great deal about yourself. Often, even the little habitual or trivial things we say and do have meaning, for they point to core beliefs that we may have not yet discovered in ourselves. For instance, look at the common expression a lot of people make when they're given a gift, and they say, "Oh, you *shouldn't* have!" Do they really mean it, or are they just trying to be grateful, or polite? These words, insignificant as they seem, may reveal a lack of self-worth, or even dishonesty. Though seemingly inconsequential, these little, habitual phrases reflect a great deal about ourselves and others.

The most important key to sustaining your relationship is to visualize the two of you together, in harmony, supporting each other, very close to one another, building a future together. If you maintain this visualization, a great many petty difficulties that arise will simply dissolve of their own accord, not all (we'll work with other methods later that deal with bigger problems), but a great many. When petty difficulties become exaggerated, they begin to look like major obstacles, but they are, in fact, insignificant problems that can easily be dissolved over time with a positive mental attitude.

This is not merely "positive thinking," a method that too often ignores the negative things in life. It is very important to deal with all the problems and difficulties that arise in a long-term relationship as openly as possible. This can be done when there is a strong underlying visualization of a successful relationship, where the problems are going to be worked out for the greatest good of everyone involved.

It also helps to visualize feeling good about yourself, about your body, your capabilities, your goals and dreams. Visualize that you have a good, strong self-image. Once your relationship is established, don't fall into the trap of laziness or complacency by letting your positive self-image fade. Be aware, also, of the trap of viewing your lover in a negative light, being constantly aware of every fault and shortcoming. Too often relationships suffer because one partner has become highly critical of the other; this attitude becomes a continual reflection of one another's weaknesses. The antidote is to focus on each other's *strengths*, to see that person once again as being capable, attractive, and desirable. Visualization makes this transformation possible for anyone, in any situation.

Keep on the sunny side of your relationship. You don't need to deny any part of yourself or your partner, or any of your feelings. Simply take time now and then to count your blessings, to be grateful for what you have, to remember each other's strengths, and to realize that your relationship is mutually satisfying and supportive for both of you.

Too often a couple will focus so much on their problems and difficulties that they forget the happiness and mutual appreciation that brought them together in the first place. It is only after they have drifted apart, sometimes very painfully, that they begin to remember once again all the good things they shared together. This is a typical example of what has been called the "half-empty glass syndrome," where life is compared to a half-empty glass of water. Some people continually focus on the half that *isn't there:* they see what is wrong with something before recognizing what is good about it. When we are caught in this kind of attitude, we spend far too much time complaining about our limitations and problems — the "empty" half of the glass. Unfortunately, this visualization, like all others, tends to be self-fulfilling. "Argue for your limitations, and they are yours."

Through conscious thought and with practice, we can learn to focus on the half of the glass that is *full* — learning to see the good in our relationships first, and then and only then dealing with what needs improvement.

Which half of the glass do you usually focus on? Answer that honestly. If you need to, do this exercise, repeatedly, if necessary:

> *Visualize and list all the good things about yourself, your lover, and your relationship together. Do it in your own way, in your own words.*

*Then take some time in your life to enjoy these
things, and to express your appreciation both to yourself and to your lover.*

You are unique, as are your friends and lovers and
the things you all share together. Why not enjoy it, and
live your life to the fullest?

Creating a Satisfying Relationship

By repeating a clear visualization until it becomes
strongly rooted in our consciousness, present even when
we're not consciously aware of it, we can truly create a
fully satisfying romantic relationship, even an "ideal"
relationship. This use of the word 'ideal' may seem un-
realistic, but in visualization we are allowed to be un-
realistic, to create what is absolutely perfect for us. (As
James Allen wrote, "Your vision is the promise of what
you shall one day be.") The relationship that actually
evolves from this visualization may not exactly match our
expectations, but that doesn't mean it can't be our ideal
relationship: we simply have to expand our views of what
is ideal for us.

While clear and specific visualization is important,
it is also necessary to be very flexible in order to create
satisfying relationships. Don't limit yourself to specific
expectations about your lover or yourself; don't wait for
this "ideal" package to appear in order to have the relationship you desire. The trick is to be very specific in
asking for what you want, and very flexible in dealing
with what you get.

As a relationship grows over time, situations are bound
to arise when you feel that you or your lover is acting in
less than an "ideal" way. The more you get to know each

other, becoming familiar with each other's differences, the more you become aware of each other's faults and shortcomings. This can be irritating, because you may have to change your own habits to accommodate your partner's ways, or you may have to accept something you once felt was unacceptable. For example, one of you may be neater than the other, and so feel the other is too sloppy. One may be more organized, one wants to go out more often, or travel more. One may want to read while the other prefers to watch TV. One may work harder and be more ambitious so that the other seems lazier in contrast. The list could go on forever.

Many of these differences are inevitable as two people get to know each other and invariably grow and change. This hardly seems to be the stuff of which "ideal" relationships are made. Yet, with a strong, positive visualization and effective communication, these differences can be dealt with in a way that results in a deep, true satisfaction for both people.

Flexibility and Unconditional Love

Successful relationships require a degree of flexibility; those involved need to develop the willingness and ability to let the other person fully be themselves. This is easy for some and difficult for others. If your lover doesn't feel like fixing the screen door or cleaning the bathroom or making love or doing something they promised to do, try not to react negatively. Instead, do your best to allow them to do what they want to do. If you find yourself reacting negatively, try to let your anger go as soon as possible. It does no good to blame your lover, or to carry a grudge. Both you and your lover need permission to fail in fulfilling commitments now and then, and you both must be allowed to change your mind and your plans. In an ideal relationship, there has to be room for spontaneous and impetuous action, even if it means not doing something which one of you promised to do.

Albert Einstein has been credited with this statement: "Women marry men hoping they will change, and men marry women hoping they will not. So each is inevitably disappointed." If he did actually say this, it is one instance in which I completely disagree with him. I hope he was joking (although most jokes reflect a *serious* core belief). Disappointment in a relationship is certainly *not* inevitable, it is simply up to each of us to make sure we are not disappointed. Our challenge is to grow enough and become mature enough to be flexible and learn to accept change in ourselves and our partners. Change is inevitable, so we may as well learn to accept it. Yet, if our partners do *not* change according to our expectations, this has to be accepted as well. We can never change others; we can only offer our honest opinions and hope that others will eventually change themselves. Persuasion is fine, but manipulation, in the long run, does not work.

Flexibility and acceptance are important ingredients in creating the kind of love that always grows in an ever-exciting way: the love which is *unconditional*. Unconditional love is pure and total acceptance of a person as they are at every moment. Every mother feels it for her child; every lover feels it during the first intense, exhilarating moments of mutual attraction. But all too often, unconditional love fades, and is unknowingly replaced by *conditional* love, a love that basically says, "I will love you if you change in this way," or "I will love you if you do this for me." Conditional love is not given with pure and total acceptance; there are strings attached, pressures, obligations. Conditional love is ineffective in forcing change, just as all manipulation is, and it is destructive to any relationship.

Unconditional love can be developed, and it can be replaced if it has faded from a relationship. It requires the intention to do so and a great deal of open, honest communication. Both partners must feel free to express their feelings whenever they feel pressured by conditional love. One of the greatest results of practicing the fine art of communication, and especially of playing the communication game, is the reawakening of unconditional love for your partner. This love is certainly the most important element of any lasting relationship.

Encouraging Self-Development

All of us need time to pursue our own interests; we all need support in the ongoing process of our individual growth. Our relationships should ideally assist rather than hinder these efforts, nurturing our natural evolution, as individuals and as a species.

We all need to find time for our favorite forms of relaxation, rejuvenation, and development of personal interests and skills. These may consist of taking long solitary walks, working in the garage, taking classes, going fishing, doing exercises, working on an artistic project, or even sitting in a neighborhood bar. It is different for every individual, but whatever it is, we need to give ourselves time to be ourselves, and we need to give our lovers the same freedom.

It is essential for your happiness in the long run to allow yourself the necessary time for privacy and personal reflection in your life. It is wise to encourage others, too, to have their own time for privacy and personal reflection, to develop a healthy mutual respect for each other's private nurturing time. As Kahlil Gibran wrote so beautifully in *The Prophet,*

Let there be spaces in your togetherness,
And let the winds of heaven dance between you.
Love one another, but make not a bond of love:
Let it rather be a moving sea between the shores of
*   your souls.*
Fill each other's cup but drink not from one cup...
Sing and dance together and be joyous, but let each
*   of you be alone,*
Even as the strings of a lute are alone though they
*   quiver with the same music...*
And stand together yet not too near together:
For the pillars of the temple stand apart,
And the oak tree and the cypress grow not in each
*   other's shadow.*[3]

You are separate individuals; each of you should encourage the other to develop to the fullest potential, providing each other with the support to do what is necessary to fulfill yourselves. Don't fall into the trap of being overly critical if your lover doesn't share your interests and passions and skills, or doesn't do what you would expect. Don't try to force your lover into an unsuitable career or hobby; allow them to find their own avenues of self-expression. If your lover has an art, hobby, or other deep personal interest, provide as much support as possible; give appreciation and even assistance when necessary. If your lover has no special interest or passion, you can still provide the time (it may be years) and the opportunity for self-discovery.

Encouraging self-development — helping yourself and others discover the means to true self-fulfillment — is the solution to the boredom or sense of inadequacy so many face when their lovers or children leave them, whether temporarily or permanently. There's no good reason to ever feel bored; boredom is merely an indication that you haven't been giving yourself enough time to focus on and develop your own personal interests. People who are growing and developing are never bored, and never in the unfortunate situation of being totally dependent on someone else for their fulfillment and happiness.

Love

Love is the short, sweet, simple name we give to a vast array of complex and profound emotions. All the artists of the world will never reflect it completely; all the writers of all time will never describe it fully; our greatest scientists will never understand it in its entirety.

Love is vast, love is mystical, love is powerful, capable of transforming us into higher beings on the evolutionary scale. Gerald Jampolsky has said that love is letting go of fear.[4] Think about that for a moment; it's a fresh perspective, deep and meaningful.

Leo Buscaglia, in his book *Love*, says "Love is always open arms. If you close your arms about love you will find that you are left holding only yourself."[5] Think about that one for a moment, too. It's undeniably true.

The purpose of this book is to help people create and sustain the relationships they want. In order to do this, we need to closely examine the nature of love, and learn to distinguish between two very different kinds of love that characterize almost every romantic relationship.

The first is a love that most of us are already familiar with, and a great many of us pursue: the initial, euphoric feeling of romantic love. This is often called "falling in love," yet it is much more like "soaring in love." The feeling can be one of the greatest experiences in life; it is powerful enough to temporarily dissolve all of our difficulties, and make life seem exhilarating.

When this feeling happens, take full advantage of it, luxuriate in it, experience it to the fullest. It is a gift that appears unexpectedly, and vanishes unexpectedly as well, for it is fleeting, and cannot be grasped and held onto forever. Unfortunately, the feeling is so sweet that many of us want to sustain it, especially after it has dissolved. But that is like wishing for a rainbow to reappear or a brilliant moment in a sunset to last for a lifetime. Romantic love is ephemeral, and it won't last.

This feeling is often taken as an indication of a successful relationship, and when the feeling inevitably dissolves, the relationship may then seem unsatisfying. When this occurs, we miss seeing the far greater, lasting potential of yet another kind of love.

This second kind of love can be called *sustained romantic love*. In some ways, it is the exact opposite of euphoric romantic love, for it develops only over a relatively long period of time. It is deep and lasting, and grows deeper with the passing years. This mature love forms a bond which powerfully supports both people. It is certainly one of the greatest miracles of this universe we live in, for this kind of love is eternal, lasting even after that transition we call death. It is vast, it is mystical.

Sustained romantic love *can* be attained and nurtured. It is a love that can be cultivated. When we find ourselves in sustained romantic love, we grow as individuals and enjoy a far more satisfying life experience for its presence.

The Great Importance of "Little Things"

It has been said so often that it is a cliche, although certainly a true one: little things mean a lot. All too frequently during the course of a long-term relationship, one person will become starved for the little signs of affection that the other person could give so easily. Even an affectionate phrase now and then can be so meaningful — an affectionate phrase a day keeps the marriage counselor away. Simple, affectionate gestures can mean so much: touching a hand or stroking a cheek, kissing an ear, giving a single flower, saying "I love you" — there are at least a million little things that can be done. Brushing each other's hair occasionally, or scrubbing each other's back in the tub or shower provides soothing and affectionate physical contact.

Those who truly enjoy life enjoy such simple but significant gestures, the little things that every moment has to offer. Whether alone or with the one you love, you can focus on cultivating the fine art of enjoying life's small pleasures. A single flower, a simple poem left on the kitchen table — these little things can mean so much, for they are a testament to your love and affection.

> *It's just the little things, sometimes*
> *Like opening the refrigerator and finding*
> *A wine bottle filled with cold lemonade*
> *It's just the little things, sometimes*
> *That make me love you so*[6]

Meaningful Gestures

In enjoying the little pleasures of life, don't overlook the larger things, as well, which celebrate your togetherness. Whether for an anniversary, or for no special reason, be sure to share an occasional evening of special togeth-erness. Go out to dinner; do something extravagant. Whatever you choose, be sure to toast each other and celebrate your relationship. Trading rings can also be a lasting, significant gesture, whether or not you decide to legally marry. Treat each other to flowers and jewelry as often as possible.

Especially when money is tight, it can happen that one or both of the people in a relationship will forget to reward their lover with some token of affection. But it isn't necessary to spend much money — it's the intention that counts. At one point, years ago, when I had very little money, I bought my lover a simple silver band for a grand total of two dollars. She wears it to this day, on occasion, and somehow its simplicity makes it all the more touching and meaningful.

Napoleon once claimed that soldiers are much more motivated by medals and other baubles than by stirring speeches and causes and ideals and patriotism. There is a lot of truth in this, and it applies to our relationships as well: a piece of jewelry or a whimsical gift can mean a great deal and become a real treasure over the years. It is an acknowledgement, an affirmation in physical form, of the lasting good in your relationship.

Other Considerations

There are many other things to deal with in most long-term intimate relationships; among these are the possibility of marriage, the nature of jealousy and guilt, the fear of separation, and the healthiest way to view your partner and your relationship. Every one of us needs to carefully examine these things in light of the changing times in which we live.

Marriage, and Other Possibilities

Marriage is certainly one of the most meaningful statements a couple can make together. The ritual formalizes long-term commitment to one another. One of the best recent developments in our society has been the gradual disintegration of the complete dominance of the so-called 'nuclear family' over every other possible way of living. Previously, a great deal of pressure was exerted on *everyone* to live in the same social pattern, consisting of husband, wife, and children. Now, finally, due to the sheer number of people breaking the mold, a wide variety of alternatives are available for you and me. The only requirement now is that you discover for yourself your most appropriate lifestyle and give yourself permission to live it.

This makes marriage even more attractive than it ever was, because most people who get married today do so because they want to, not because they have to. There may be areas of the country, and there are certainly parts of the world, where this is not yet true, where people are still being pressured into marriage against their wishes or better judgment. But in many areas of this country today, the tremendous social pressure that demands marriage no longer exists.

As we grow and mature, as we discover, and hopefully live, a life directed solely by personal choice and rooted in our personal "moral freedom," we learn, through our successes and mistakes, to develop the social arrangement that works best for us. We come to realize that *every* lifestyle has its advantages and disadvantages, and no one choice is inherently better than any other.

Living alone, for example, has a great many advantages. I've thoroughly enjoyed it when I've done it, and I look back on those times as important periods of growth and self-discovery, periods that changed the course of my life, and brought me much closer to my dreams, ideals, goals, and purposes. Looking back, I can see it was necessary for me to live alone for a while in order to discover who I was and what I wanted in life.

One of the greatest advantages of living alone is that your time is all your own; no one intrudes on you without an invitation. Your physical space is all your own, and you can make a mess or do whatever you want to do without blame or criticism. The main disadvantage of living alone, on the other hand, is loneliness. No one greets you when you come home; there's no one to relax with or spend the evening with in casual conversation. This loneliness can be overcome, however, with some inner work and some examination of core beliefs.

Living unmarried with roommates and/or lovers has its advantages and disadvantages, as well. Companionship is readily available, yet there is still freedom to change the arrangement when and if you feel like it. There are relatively few restrictions or long-term commitments, yet there are times when your personal space is disturbed. A live-in arrangement, compared to marriage, is similar in some ways to renting, as opposed to buying, a house. You have to consider the fact that you're not necessarily investing your time to build something as solid or permanent as those who marry are attempting to build.

Marriage is the most universal and enduring form of romantic love relationships. The act of making a lifelong commitment to another person creates a bond that transcends both of you. A married couple creates a whole which is much greater than the sum of its parts, and this strength and relative stability are ideal for a great many people.

Another important advantage in marriage, for a lot of people, is that the focus of attention shifts from being self-centered to taking on a greater responsibility that includes someone else. Living for someone else, as well as for yourself, can have a very positive effect on many people.

As in every other arrangement, there are also disadvantages to marriage. In getting married, you are committed to one person, and to working it out successfully with that one person or else spending your life in compromise where one or both of you is not getting what you need from the relationship. In marriage, you've got to learn to communicate with each other, and work out difficulties. Resentment, even over insignificant things, can build up over the course of a marriage and become very destructive to the happiness of both partners. If you find you are out of alignment on some things — after all, you're very different individuals — you have to accept this and resolve it in a way that works for both of you.

There are, of course, many other advantages and disadvantages to marriage, and all the other possible living arrangements. If you are not certain which arrangement is best for you, you need to do some honest self-examination. Sit down and list all the advantages and disadvantages you can think of for every possibility open to you. Spend some time with this, weighing every possibility as carefully as you can. The more thought you give to each alternative, and the more deeply you examine your feelings before making a decision, the better are your chances for being happy with the arrangement.

To marry or not to marry, to live alone or with someone else — the choice is entirely up to you, and you alone.

The Key to a Happy Marriage

A friend of mine met a couple who had been happily married for over 50 years. She asked them for the secret of their success and the woman replied, with a laugh, "He spoils me rotten!" Her husband laughed and said, "She takes pretty good care of me, too!"

That, in a nutshell, is the key to a happy marriage. Most of us are grappling with core beliefs about our incapacity to truly love, to truly give. These beliefs are usually the most difficult thing to deal with in long-term relationships. But if you find somebody to love, someone to put on a pedestal, someone to "spoil rotten," and give them what they want, you'll discover that you *do* know how to truly love.

As it says in a Native American marriage blessing some good friends of mine used at the end of their marriage ceremony:

> *Now you will feel no rain, for each of you will be shelter for the other.*

> *Now you will feel no cold, for each of you will be warmth for the other.*

> *Now there is no more loneliness; you are two persons, but there is only one life before you.*

*Go now to your dwelling, to enter into the days
of your life together,*

*And may your days be good and long upon the
earth.*

Jealousy, and Other "Negative" Emotions

Jealousy is one of the most challenging problems to be faced in a long-term relationship. Not too long ago, it was fashionable to attempt to do away with jealousy. Popular writers and teachers told us it could be transcended, or "reprogrammed," and a lot of people tried to build relationships that were free of jealousy. I know I tried.

The only problem was that it didn't work, at least not in my experience or in the experience of others I know who tried it. In fact, for quite awhile I thought I had gone beyond jealousy. Then I discovered I hadn't gone beyond it, but had simply not created a situation in quite a while that made me jealous. Once the situation arose, when I found my lover had suddenly become infatuated with another man, I was as jealous as ever.

I've since come to feel that jealousy is natural, and perhaps inevitable, at our current level of evolution, and cannot and should not be ignored or suppressed. The first healthy step in dealing with all of our so-called "negative feelings," such as anger, jealousy, and fear, is to completely accept them. We're okay, and our feelings are okay. This does not mean we have license to act upon these feelings in a way that hurts other people; it simply means that we have to honestly accept our feelings as they arise, and not try to reject them, ignore them, suppress them, or pretend they don't exist.

Once we thoroughly accept the wide range of our feelings, the next step we must take is to honestly assess the intensity of those feelings. Undoubtedly, a certain *moderate* degree of jealousy, anger, or fear is natural in even the most balanced, sane, and enlightened people. Show me a person who says he or she feels no jealousy, anger, or fear and I'll show you someone who's deluded, and denying their own feelings. As long as you experience these feelings in a moderate degree, simply accept and live with them, and then get on with the rest of your life.

Problems arise when these feelings get out of control, when they become *excessive*. Mere acceptance is not enough; this is when we need to confront and resolve these emotions. If anger, fear, or jealousy ever dominates our lives to the extent that we regret our actions, or find our ability to have satisfying relationships, productive jobs, or an enjoyable life experience hampered, then it is time to take action.

Our range of choices is vast. The core belief process and the visualization techniques given earlier can be very effective in dealing with detrimental emotions. Sometimes just talking very honestly with a good friend can help release these destructive pent-up feelings. Sometimes friends can provide very good suggestions on how to best handle these feelings, for our friends often see us much more clearly than we do. If working on yourself or consulting friends doesn't help, there are many other people you can turn to. Never be afraid to ask for help if you need it. It doesn't mean you are bad, or weak; on the contrary, it takes strength and courage to admit our problems, and it takes maturity and wisdom to seek help in solving them. We should never be ashamed to ask for help when we need it.

There are many excellent books on the subject; there are a great many therapists, counselors, teachers, and others in the helping professions who are capable of working with emotional disturbances. There are classes and workshops in every major city and in a great many small towns as well. One of the best things I ever did to constructively deal with my anger, for instance, was to take a short, three-evening course on assertiveness training. It taught me a lot about effective communication.

But to return to jealousy, specifically: some jealousy is usually present in intimate relationships, but something should be done about it only if it starts hurting the relationship. I've known completely monogamous couples who have kept their agreement not to have sexual relations with others, and yet one of the partners became so jealous that they didn't really want the other partner to do anything without them. The situation, of course, became frustrating and suffocating for both of them. Insinuating questions were asked if they came home from work a bit late, or if they went to meet a friend for coffee. This kind of jealousy is excessive and must be effectively resolved before the relationship can grow and thrive.

The saddest thing about excessive jealousy is that it tends to create that which it fears. I've known of several relationships that ended precisely because those involved were neurotically worried that their partner would leave, and these fears affected the quality of the relationship so much that it finally happened! A classic case of a fearful, repeated visualization that comes true.

Minor doses of jealousy, anger, or fear are not bad; we might as well consider them good, because these emotions are here to stay, and we certainly have to learn to live with them. In doing so, we're bound to learn more about ourselves, and become better people for it. It's only the excessive, dominating emotions that have to be dealt with, using definite, strong action.

Guilt

Far too many of us have spent too much time and energy wallowing in excessive guilt. This is an emotion that must be understood and dealt with before we can discover our own form of "moral freedom" and before we can create successful relationships.

There are two kinds of guilt: *natural* guilt and *conditioned* (or imposed) guilt.[7] Natural guilt is useful and necessary; conditioned guilt is harmful and unnecessary, and can be overcome, just as we can overcome extreme anger, jealousy, or fear.

Natural guilt is felt when your intuitive sense tells you that you have done something that violates *your own moral code*. Everyone of us has a personal moral code. Its nature varies among different individuals, and this is why you can't tell others what is right for them, and why a government can't successfully legislate morality. History certainly proves that this is futile (though our government still tries, and fails, to do so).

Whenever we violate our own moral code, we feel it. It is a strong feeling that can't be ignored, unless we take extreme measures to completely desensitize our feelings. This feeling is a message to ourselves, a reminder not to repeat the mistake, that the action is not good for us, not in alignment with our goals and purposes in life.

Natural guilt may be severe for a relatively short time, if the act was severe enough. It serves the useful purpose of getting us back on course, and preventing us from being self-destructive. But natural guilt is not *chronic* and will not continue over a long period of time, unless we repeat the actions that violate our moral code. Natural guilt has a message for us; it delivers the message, and then evaporates.

Conditioned, or imposed guilt, on the other hand, may linger for months or even years after an event. This is the guilt we have developed because others have convinced us we should have it — *not* because it violates our own moral code. It can cause a great deal of emotional damage unless we learn to see that it is purely conditioned, unnatural, and harmful for us. It can destroy our joy of living. Conditioned guilt is a powerful tool which is used by far too many parents, teachers, churches, and other people and social organizations in an attempt to control people. It is used so widely because it has proven to be so effective.

Fortunately, it is not necessary to be controlled by conditioned guilt. When we tune into our natural, intuitive feelings, we can always discover the right choice, and in acting on that choice, we know we have chosen rightly, because it feels completely in alignment with our greatest purposes in life. Lingering conditioned guilt can be discarded through visualization and affirmations, or therapy, if necessary.

Contrary to some popular conditioned beliefs, we are not condemned to be guilty creatures for life, even though we may choose to break the rules and live as we really want to live. We are meant to be naturally healthy and happy, and to fulfill a unique purpose in life which has to do with our creative abilities, our individual talents and passions.

Separation

The intention of this book is to help you create and sustain the kind of relationships you want, so why is a section on separation included? The possibility of separation exists in every relationship, and it must be considered, not hidden in a dark mental closet.

There are two kinds of separation to consider: unintentional and intentional. Each type has its own unique pain, and each can be a time of new discovery and personal growth.

Unintentional separation is the result of either death or unexpected separation initiated by the other person. When unintentional separation occurs, it is crucial to take adequate time to grieve and heal. The aftermath of such separation has three distinct stages, and the intense emotions in each of these stages must be fully accepted.[8] The first stage involves shock, disbelief, and denial. Particularly in a case of sudden death, the immediate reaction, after the initial shock has passed, is to deny that it happened. Perhaps it is all a bad dream, and you will soon awaken, and things will be as they used to be.

This stage is soon followed by the grief and anger typical of the second stage. The haunting question "Why did it happen to *me?*" is a common reaction in this stage. This is the most important stage to fully accept and allow yourself to experience completely, without denial. Too often well-intentioned friends urge the grieving person to move through this stage quickly, to forget the pain as soon as possible, accept the loss and get on with the normal routines of life. But the grieving process is natural and necessary, and must be allowed to run its course. This stage may be as short as a few months or as long as several years; it varies widely with different people. In order to be fully healed, no one should ever be pressured to spend either more or less time than is necessary in grieving for a loved one.

The third stage is acceptance, the final, complete acceptance which comes in the wake of experiencing grief fully. It allows the person to become whole again, to resume a normal life, fully healed, ready and willing for a new relationship with its new and different challenges.

Intentional separation has become very common in our society today. Fifty percent of our marriages end in divorce; in some parts of the country there have been more divorces than marriages filed in some years. As I have said before, this is not necessarily bad, even though it can be a painful experience. Today we no longer have to compromise in a marriage relationship. If we are not getting what we need from our relationship, in spite of the fact that we have made every effort, using the communication and visualization processes given earlier, then we must make a decision either to accept the relationship as it is, though we may not get what we want or need, or leave the relationship.

Oscar Wilde once said, "Divorces are made in heaven." It is a flippant remark, as most of his remarks were, but it contains a kernel of truth. Just as marriages are made in heaven, in the sense that they offer the possibility of the lasting happiness of a solid, committed relationship, divorces can also be said to be made in heaven because they terminate unsuccessful relationships and hold the promise of a new, successful relationship.

We all deserve relationships that are supportive, loving, and satisfying, but we must create such a relationship; no one can do it for us. But if, in spite of your best efforts, your relationship is not fulfilling your needs, don't be afraid to consider separation.

As long as you continue to visualize what you want and need, and practice the fine art of communication with those you meet, you are bound to create the kind of relationship you want, sooner or later.

Letting Go of Resentment

Many of us prevent ourselves from creating a successful, sustained relationship because we have not let go of resentment and anger left over from earlier relationships. These feelings may have arisen in our first marriage, or be caused by some unpleasant or traumatic experience, such as rape or incest, or they may even come from the distant past: we may feel a deep resentment toward one or both of our parents and carry this feeling around for many years, sometimes even for our entire lifetime. These feelings affect every other relationship we create. Resentful, angry feelings, whether generated today, yesterday, or in the distant past, can ruin even the best relationships.

The simple healing technique of *letting go* can do wonders for this kind of anger and resentment. The more formal religious term for this process is *forgiveness*. There are many ways to let go, to forgive. Simply relax and visualize the object of your resentment or anger, and then affirm to them, repeatedly, the following: "I release you, forgive you, and let you go," or "I now let go of all old conditions and relationships," or "All that has offended me, I now forgive." Find the words that have the strongest resonance for you.

The specific words and even the methods you use do

not really matter, but it is very important to come to terms within yourself with people who have hurt you, so you can fully accept them as they were and as they are, so you can truly let go of your feelings of anger and resentment toward them. If negative feelings continue to arise, repeat the above exercise until you have completely let go and fully forgiven. When you have, the feelings will no longer arise.

If the feelings are so strong and intense that this exercise doesn't effectively clear them, find someone, a friend or a professional, who can help you. These feelings of resentment and anger are only hurting *you*, so if you can find ways to let these feelings go, it will be for your own good. Forgive everyone, including yourself, for wrong actions, and you can start to build a meaningful relationship, without being haunted by any more ghosts from the past.

Your Greatest Teacher

Our education certainly doesn't stop when we leave school; we are constantly learning and growing, for we are evolving beings. It is healthy to see your world and your relationships as being filled with meaningful lessons, to view everyone you meet as a potential teacher. This way you will never stop learning and growing; you will never get mired in a rut of your own making.

A destructive pattern of dominance and submission may emerge in some long-term relationships. The dominant role can be played by either partner, and the dominance can take many different forms, ranging from obvious to subtle. It becomes destructive when the dominant person stops listening to the other or stops respecting the other person's abilities, and the attractions that brought them together in the first place are forgotten. We are all probably familiar with couples made up of an overly critical husband or a "nagging" wife. These common stereotypes are symptomatic of a dominant/submissive relationship, and this imbalance of power leads to frustration for both people involved.

This problem (and many others, as well) can be solved when you come to understand that *your lover is your greatest teacher*. In the broadest sense, everyone we meet is our teacher, because it is through our interaction with others that we are given an opportunity to understand ourselves more thoroughly, and to grow in the process. In this sense, some of the most difficult people we encounter can be our best teachers. Those who make us the most angry, for instance, are forcing us to see a side of ourselves we normally ignore. Yet, we learn a lot about ourselves in the process, whether we want to or not, and hopefully grow a bit wiser.

The depth and longevity of a sustained romantic relationship make our partners our finest teachers. In fact, we choose our lovers, subconsciously perhaps, to assist in our life's goals and purposes, to help us develop into more complete, aware, and fulfilled individuals. The relationship you have with your lover, whether smooth or rough, loving or argumentative, reflects qualities that you need to pay attention to. If the relationship brings out a loving, nurturing side of yourself, your lover may be helping you treat yourself better. If an angry, critical side of yourself emerges, your lover may be forcing you to confront your discontent with your surroundings and yourself.

Your lover may be reflecting habit patterns that need to be changed: perhaps a lack of consideration for others, excessive criticism and anger, a lack of organization, laziness, or failing in some other way to live up to your potential. In these cases, your lover is forcing you to see what you might otherwise ignore, and so your lover is doing you a great favor, being your finest teacher, in pointing these things out to you.

Our lovers are capable of showing us where we need to work most on ourselves in order to fully realize our potential. It can be very valuable for men, for instance, to consider their lovers as the voice of their own intuitive minds — their "intuitive consultants." While there are exceptions, in general women are more closely connected to their natural intuition than men are; men should respect this and listen carefully to a woman's intuition.

As we saw earlier, scientific research on the structure of the human brain over the past decade has demonstrated the existence of two very different brain functions: the rational, logical mind (usually located in the left hemisphere of the cerebral cortex), and the intuitive, nonlinear, "holistic" mind (usually the right hemisphere). To achieve harmony in our relationships and our lives, we need to achieve harmony within ourselves, within our own mind. We need to acknowledge and support *both sides* of ourselves equally, we need to integrate our rational side with our intuitive side. Once this is accomplished, we find that we are not only living a fulfilling life, but that our relationships are working harmoniously as well.

How do we do this? By tuning into our intuitive mind, we can learn, through trial and error, to hear its voice, follow its direction, and support its goals and visions using the power of the logic and organizational skills of our rational mind. This is what it means to be fully integrated. Why follow the intuitive mind? Because our intuitive faculties are our connection with a larger perspective; our intuitive senses are the key to our so-called "subconscious" mind, our connection with all of our past experience, and with an even greater intuitive awareness. Our intuitive side is the source of a far greater amount of information than we could ever remember rationally; our intuitive side is the source of our creative impulses and our true, innate wisdom.

The rational mind is the source of acquired knowledge and the ability to organize and consciously direct our energies. When the rational mind is in control, ignoring the subtler, broader intuitive mind, we can accomplish a great deal, but it is also easy to become severely misguided, or feel a sense of emptiness in our accomplishments. Probably the most extreme example of misguided rational activity today, activity that completely stifles intuitive feelings, is demonstrated in the proliferation of nuclear weapons by our nation and so many others. Rational thinking, uncontrolled and unguided by intuitive feelings, can lead to the destruction of ourselves and our world.

With our intuitive mind and feelings to guide us, and the organization and structure of our rational mind to assist us, we can live our lives and create our careers in full alignment with our highest purposes in life. And, in doing this, we unleash enormous inspired, creative power. Boredom, wasted time, and wasted effort become things of the past.

Women, for a number of reasons, are usually more in touch with their intuitive minds than men are. Men, for their part, can learn to listen to the words and feelings of their lovers as the voice of their own intuitive mind. However, there are times when even the most balanced, sane people become cut off from the innate wisdom of their intuitive mind. Then they needlessly worry, criticize themselves or others, make life difficult for themselves, make poor decisions, and behave in a variety of other unbalanced ways. At these times, your intuitive mind will tell you that your lover is cut off from their intuitive feedback, and can use your wisdom to get back on track.

If, in the ideal relationship, the man hears the woman as the voice of his own intuitive mind, how should the woman best view the man? Ideally, she should see him as a source of strength, awareness and support, helping her to live in accordance with her own intuitive understanding, supporting her in all that she dreams of becoming. And she should see him as an intuitive being in his own right, consulting him as much as he consults her.

In the finest, most successful relationships, each partner helps the other tune into intuitive wisdom and support it with knowledge and strength. Each person is given the opportunity and the encouragement to discover their unique purpose in life, which can only be discovered intuitively, and then supported to take the action appropriate to fulfill that purpose.

Of course, this is the ideal, the "higher side," the greatest potential, of each person involved. In the reality of day-to-day life, you may not see this side exhibited often. If you aren't getting this kind of support from your lover, give it to yourself. Not only will you become stronger and more complete, but you'll soon find that others are giving you the same support you are giving yourself.

Your Relationship is Greater than Yourself

Once you have mastered the art of sustaining a relationship, you discover a wonderful thing: your relationship is greater than the sum of its parts. It is bigger than both of you. It raises you up out of the narrow confines of endless, self-centered thinking into a broader perspective which makes your personal problems less significant.

A successful relationship actually creates a force, a power, which supports both of you in becoming better people, more active, more fulfilled. You find that your strengths complement each other, and both of you become much stronger in the process of being with each other.

When this happens, you have discovered the value of a committed relationship.

6

A BETTER WAY OF LIFE

Cherish your visions; cherish your ideals; cherish the
music that stirs in your heart, the beauty that forms
in your mind, the loveliness that drapes your highest
thoughts, for out of them will grow all delightful
conditions, all heavenly environments; of these, if you
remain true to them, your world will at last be built.[1]
—James Allen

A LL OF US have had enough experience with the core
beliefs that impede healthy, satisfying relationships
to want to find a better way that will work for each of us,
whatever that may be. Reading this book is a strong,
positive step in that direction. Now it's important to sustain the momentum you have begun, and continue to
create meaningful changes in your life.

Remember that there is always a better way, you can
always move closer to your goals; you never have to settle
for a relationship that doesn't support and fulfill you, you
don't have to accept a lifestyle that is not satisfying. You
may have to take personal risks, move into new and scary
territory, but the power to improve our condition in life
is always available if we want it enough. We are evolving

beings with the potential, the latent ability, to live in harmony and abundance in a peaceful, loving world. We *can* create a life experience for ourselves which includes loving — that is, accepting and even enjoying — *every moment* of our lives. We can spend our lives practicing and mastering the art of being a friend and a lover: loving each other, loving our work (even its problems), loving the weaknesses in ourselves and in others, and, yes, even loving our enemies.

These words have all been said and written before, but they need to be said again and again, because we keep forgetting them, personally and on national and international levels. What would this world be like if we really loved our enemies, amd everyone else? The world would change overnight. And it can be done: it's simply a matter of intention, communication, and firm and consistent visualization.

As more of us come to believe the truth of this, we can actually create such a world, because these beliefs, just like negative beliefs, are self-fulfilling. Real, measurable, positive change can occur in our lives when we start loving ourselves and others — and we don't have to wait for others to change in order to change our world, for once we change ourselves the world changes as well. When we can love our problems, a great many of those problems dissolve. When we can love our enemies, we soon discover that we have very few enemies left. It's not so difficult to love, not even to love our enemies. In fact, it's very natural to love; all we need to do is contact the intuitive, compassionate part of ourselves. All we neeed to do is emotionally *accept* others. If you have difficulty doing this, just remind yourself that, given different circumstances, you could be in the other person's situation: "There, but for fortune, goes you or me."

It is time for us all to realize that the world needs a lot more compassion and acceptance and a lot less anger and separation. Remember the words of Henry David Thoreau, quoted earlier: so many of us are still the "slaves of King Prejudice," and we won't really be free and content until we can let go of the prejudice we carry with us, and truly accept *all* others in our lives. We don't have to agree with them, but we have to accept them for what they are. I have to accept, for instance, the current leaders of our country, even though they are doing things I completely disagree with, such as building nuclear warheads and supporting governments that don't respect basic human rights. And I have to accept everyone I meet and work with in my life, though some people are terribly angry, or neurotic, or harmful, to themselves or others.

Most of all, we have to learn to accept our lovers and ourselves, just as we are. When we can give and receive honest feedback, when we can make efforts to change for the better, we act from a place of strength, feeling good about ourselves, and our weakness, doubt, or fear no longer controls our actions.

To truly accept is to truly love.

We have touched on this before, but never really stated it outright: the single best thing to remember in order to preserve your relationships is to *focus on the good in all your relationships, and in every moment of your life*. Again, this is not merely "positive thinking," which many believe to be ineffective because it only denies the negative. Instead, focusing on what is good is very effective — it can work wonders, in fact. For what we focus on is what we *see;* what we see is what we experience.

Remember the metaphor of the half-empty glass: some people immediately focus on the fact that it is half empty and feel a sense of loss. But other people look at the same glass and see that it is half full, and they feel satisfaction and fulfillment. If you can focus on the good in your relationships, that good will grow.

There is a good reason for every one of your relationships, whether that reason is clear to you or not. There is a good reason why your parents were the way they were, a good reason why you have chosen the lovers you have chosen, there is a good reason why you are doing just what you are doing, there is a good reason why you have the friends and co-workers you have, and there is a good reason why you are the person you are — physically, mentally, and emotionally. Focus on that good, and you expand that good. As you continue to focus on that good, you, your relationships, and the quality of your whole life gets better and better.

What could be more rewarding?

The Friends' Agreement

A few years ago, a relative of my lover's came to stay with us for a while. She was generally warm and friendly, but she was difficult to live with in some ways: she had a great deal of anger in her, especially toward men (originating with her father, who was violent and sadistic), she had a very low opinion of herself, and was an alchoholic and a former patient in some mental hospitals. A few days after she arrived, I was wrote the following agreement. I read it to her. She liked it and we both agreed to it.

Her visit went smoothly after that, although there were a few times when I had to remind her of the agreement, and a few times when we had some very honest and direct talks with each other. We both grew a lot in the process, and became genuinely fond of each other.

This agreement works beautifully with lovers, parents, friends, children, co-workers, in-laws, relatives — anyone you may know. Just read it to them, or give them a copy; feel free to change the wording wherever you want, as this agreement (like an affirmation) is a very personal thing.

THE FRIENDS' AGREEMENT

I want to be your friend.

As a friend, I have some things to give you, and some things to ask of you — valuable things.

First of all, I want to give you my complete acceptance of you. I like you. I feel you are fine just the way you are, and I accept you just the way you are.

And I ask that you give me your acceptance. I'm asking you to like me just the way I am, or at least to do your best to see the good in me and in my life.

Secondly, I want to give you my honest feelings. I want to be able to tell you, frankly and directly, what I think and feel about you, about the world, about everything.

And I want you to give me your honest feelings. I want to hear what you think and feel about me, about the world, about everything.

I have one more thing to ask us both, something that will make our moments together times truly worth having: I ask that we both learn to hear what we're saying to each other without denying it, defending ourselves, or putting ourselves down in any way with it...that we learn to simply hear each other, accept each other's thoughts and feelings, and absorb them for a while without reacting.

There will always be time later to respond to this feedback, but first let's take awhile to absorb what the other is saying, before we respond.

Then our response will be more intelligent, more sensible; it will reveal more clearly who we really are, and what we have the potential to become.

And our relationship will thrive.

Later, I showed this agreement to a friend, and told him how well it had worked for us. He told me a something very interesting: he said that when reading it, he was reminded of a story he had heard about the renowned teacher, G.I. Gurdjieff[2]. Apparently, Gurdjieff was brash and impulsive as a young man. When his father was dying, he told the young Gurdjieff he had one favor to ask of him: whenever anyone said something to him that made him angry or caused any kind of negative response, his father asked him to wait *twenty-four hours* before replying or responding in any way to that person. Then he could respond in any way that he felt was appropriate.

Gurdjieff said that one bit of instruction changed his entire life. His father must have been a very wise man, for in his dying request he gave his son an important key to successful relationships. Once we can learn to listen to others, without immediately reacting, two very important things happen: (1) we learn to take in and absorb what others are saying, giving ourselves time to reflect on whether their words have meaning for us or not, and (2) when we finally do respond, the response is better for all concerned if it has been thought over a bit. Gurdjieff's father's advice is a key not only for successful relationships, but for a successful life.

Five Keys to Successful Relationships

Can the keys to successful relationships be summed up so neatly in five simple statements? Perhaps, but then the statements are not that simple: they each require effort, understanding, and practice. These keys have each been presented elsewhere in this book; if you need to, go back and reread and reflect on them, and then apply them to yourself.

You have the power, the ability within you, to create and sustain the relationships you want in your life. In order to do so, five things are necessary:

(1) Define what you want. You will never achieve what you want in life until you define it, clearly, precisely. Spell it out, on paper, if necessary. Stay focused on this goal, without hesitation, clearly defined in your mind. Visualize what you want in life, and keep your visualization strong.

(2) Discover and transform your core beliefs, clearing away any psychological blocks that stand in your way. You can get what you want in life, and you deserve what you want in life. Not having what you want is a sign that you are blocking yourself in some way. These blocks can be cleared, with some inner work. Take an honest look at the deep inner beliefs that prevent you from creating what you want in life, and do something to change these beliefs. It can be done, with the techniques given in this book.

(3) Practice the fine art of communication, especially by playing the communication game when necessary. Truly effective communication allows you to hear what the other person is saying, without denying it, defending yourself, or feeling hurt or guilty; it allows you to express yourself fully, without withholding anything; and it allows you to reach agreements which are satisfactory to both of you. Effective communication empowers everyone involved to be themselves, to express themselves fully, and to come to understand everyone else's point of view. And it leads to a final agreement which is fully acceptable to everyone.

(4) Learn to love, which means to accept. At the beginning and end of every successful relationship is acceptance. First of all, accept yourself, as you are this moment and as you have always been. Then accept all others in your life. Each of us has a unique way of living, of seeing things, of expressing ourselves, and every successful, long-term relationship has one thing in common: each person involved has accepted the other, as they are. Every one of us is a naturally loving being in our essence, beyond our negative core beliefs and our so-called negative emotions.

(5) Keep the visualization of your success strong. Visualize yourself and your partner as being wonderfully, ideally together, in a loving and satisfying way. Focus on the good in your relationship, remembering the good things that brought you together in the first place. Don't forget that it is all too easy to get locked into habitual patterns in which you constantly see another's weaknesses and shortcomings, and take their good qualities for granted, to such a degree that you don't even recognize them until it's too late. Keep reminding yourself of the good, positive qualities of both your lover and yourself.

By working with these five keys, you are well on your way to mastering the fine art of creating and sustaining the relationships you want in your life. It can be done. It's up to you to do it, and you alone.

The rewards are well worth the effort.

NOTES

Opening quote:
1. Rainer Maria Rilke, *Letters to a Young Poet* (New York: Random House, 1984), pp. 68-69. I have edited it slightly.

Introduction:
1. Jacqueline Simenaur, *Singles: The New Americans* (New York: Simon & Schuster, 1982).
2. Will Whittle, *How to Stop Believing in War* (Los Altos, CA: New World Library, 1984).

Chapter One:
1. James Allen, *As a Man Thinketh* (World), p. 11 and p. 13. There are a great many editions of this little gem of a book — after all, it has been in print for over 100 years. I have edited it somewhat.
2. The two most effective books dealing with the subject of core beliefs that I have discovered are: Shakti Gawain, *Creative Visualization* (Mill Valley, CA: Whatever Publishing, 1978), and Shakti Gawain, *The Creative Visualization Workbook* (Mill Valley, CA: Whatever Publishing, 1982).
3. Many of these core beliefs are quoted, with permission, from Shakti Gawain's *Creative Visualization* (see above).
4. The "core belief process" is adapted from *The Creative Visualization Workbook* by Shakti Gawain (see above).
5. The best-known and most detailed book on the subject is *The Psychology of Consciousness* by Robert Ornstein (New York: Harcourt Brace, 1977).
6. Richard Bach, *Jonathan Livingston Seagull*.
7. I read this quote in one of Catherine Ponder's excellent books, probably *Pray and Grow Rich* (Parker Publishing, 1968).

Chapter Two:
1. James Allen, *As a Man Thinketh* (World), p. 41 and p. 47.

Chapter Three:
1. James Allen (see above), p. 68.

Chapter Four:
1. Marc Allen, *Seeds to the Wind* (Mill Valley, CA: Whatever Publishing, 1979), p. 31.
2. Henry David Thoreau, *Walden* (New York: New American Library, 1973).
3. Special acknowledgement and thanks to Shirley Luthman for so

clearly pointing out our three common reactions when we hear something we don't want to hear: in her words, denying it, defending it, and "beating ourselves up." She is author of *Intimacy: The Essence of Male and Female* (Mehetabel & Co., 1977), among others.

Chapter Five:
1. James Allen (see above), pp. 68-69.
2. Rainer Maria Rilke (see above), pp. 34-35.
3. Kahlil Gibran, *The Prophet* (New York, Alfred Knopf, 1970), pp. 15-16.
4. Gerald Jampolsky, *Love is Letting Go of Fear* (Millbrae, CA: Celestial Arts, 1979).
5. Leo Buscaglia, *Love* (New York: Fawcett, 1982).
6. This is a little poem I wrote and left on the kitchen table for my lover to find. (My editor, Kim Peterson, insisted I document the source of this poem.)
7. Jane Roberts, *The Nature of Personal Reality* (New York: Prentice Hall, 1974). Has an excellent section on the nature of guilt.
8. I heard someone on a radio interview tell about the three stages of grief that are necessary to go through. I *think* it was Betty Bethards, who has written some fine books — but I'm not entirely sure.

Chapter Six:
1. James Allen (see above), pp. 67-68.
2. G.I. Gurdjieff was a well-known writer and teacher from Russia who lived during the first half of this century. He wrote, among other books, *Meetings with Remarkable Men* (New York: Dutton, 1975).

BY THE AUTHOR

Books

Tantra for the West — A Guide to Personal Freedom

Reunion — Tools for Transformation

Astrology for the New Age — An Intuitive Approach

Seeds to the Wind — Poems, Songs, Meditations

Chrysalis

Cassettes

Stress Reduction and Creative Meditations

Music

Solo Flight (solo piano)

Quiet Moments (solo piano)

Breathe (with Jon Bernoff on vibes)

Petals (with Jon Bernoff, Teja Bell, and Dallas Smith)

BOOKS TO IMPROVE YOUR LIFE
From Whatever Publishing

Work With Passion—How to Do What You Love For a Living by Nancy Anderson, career consultant. This book shows you how to develop a career doing what you really love to do. This has been called *the* career book of the eighties!

Living in the Light by Shakti Gawain. Shows us a new way of life—becoming a channel for the creative power of the universe by developing our intuition. An inspirational yet practical guide for expanding our perspective on who we are and what we have the potential to become.

Anybody Can Write—A Playful Approach by Jean Bryant. A delightful, humorous, and *effective* new book for non-writers, beginners, and writers who are "blocked." It will inspire you to learn to "fingerpaint with words," and encourage you to experience the pleasure and fulfillment of writing.

Creative Visualization by Shakti Gawain. Simple, practical, powerful techniques for creating everything you want in life. So clear and effective you can't help but experience immediate benefits. Over 500,000 copies in print.

The Creative Visualization Workbook by Shakti Gawain. Takes you step-by-step through many of the most effective techniques for dramatically improving your life in the areas of relationships, work and career, prosperity, health and beauty, and more.

CASSETTES TO IMPROVE YOUR LIFE

Living in the Light. In this powerful hour-long interview, Shakti Gawain reveals the main principles and techniques from her book of the same title, showing us how to connect with our intuition and become a creative channel for personal and planetary transformation.

Stress Reduction and Creative Meditations. Marc Allen guides you through a deeply relaxing, stress-reducing experience on the first side. Side Two contain effective, creative meditations for health, abundance, and fulfilling relationships. Background music by Jon Bernoff.

Creative Visualization. Shakti Gawain guides you through some of the most powerful and effective meditations and techniques from her book.

ORDERING INFORMATION

We invite you to send for a free copy of our full-color catalogue so that you can see our complete selection of books and cassettes.

Whatever Publishing, Inc.
P.O. Box 13257, Northgate Station
San Rafael, CA 94913
(415) 472-2100

ORDER TOLL FREE WITH YOUR VISA/MC
(800) 227-3900
(800) 632-2122 in California

ABOUT THE AUTHOR

Marc Allen has had a widely varied and fascinating education, chronicled in his book, *Chrysalis*, emphasizing both western humanistic psychology and eastern philosophies. He writes about what he lives in daily life, and his books have been enthusiastically endorsed by Elisabeth Kubler-Ross, Marilyn Ferguson, Virginia Satir, and many others.

He is also a well-known composer and keyboard artist who has recorded several albums of his music.

He lives and works in the San Francisco Bay area.